How to Make Christianity Real

by Morris Venden

Concerned Communications
Highway 59 North
Siloam Springs, Arkansas 72761

CONTENTS

1

The Most Important Question Ever Asked

What is the most important question you've ever asked? When asked about his most important question, Daniel Webster said it had to do with his accountability to God. But I can think of times in my life when the most important question of the moment was merely, "Where am I going to get enough money for an ice cream cone?"

Perhaps you've experienced this, too. I remember taking a test to become an amateur radio operator and then staying awake all night, waiting for my license to come. My most important question was, "When will my license come so I can go on the air and talk to other 'hams'?"

The most important questions of those living in famine-stricken parts of the world might be, "Where is the next morsel of food going to come from?" Other serious questions facing us might be, "Where am I going to get a new car?" or "How am I going to meet the next payments?" Granted, those are big questions. But the **most important** question about life must be asked in reference to eternity.

I'd like to reason with you for a little while and appeal to your common sense.

I heard about a Scottish lad who went home one day and said, "I've decided to be a preacher."

His wise old grandfather replied, "Son, there are three things you'll need for that. You'll need learnin', you'll need the grace of God, and you'll need common sense. If you don't have learnin', you can study for that, and if you don't have the grace of

God, you can pray for it. But if you don't have common sense, then go back to hoeing potatoes, because neither God nor man can use you as a preacher."

The wisest man in the world described the kind of wisdom that really counts: "Get wisdom, get understanding .... Wisdom is the principal thing; therefore get wisdom: and with all thy getting get understanding"—Proverbs 4:5, 7. A lot of us have more common sense than we exhibit, and we ought to use every inch of common sense we have, because without it, all the wisdom in the world isn't worth much.

One way in which many of us fail to use common sense is in our perspective on life. The old expression "we can't see the forest for the trees" seems to include at least this idea: that it is possible to become so absorbed in the details that we forget the total picture—to become so obsessed with "now" that we forget about "later." This can be done in school, lifework, and in social activities.

It's easy to become bogged down with the narrow picture of our lives here, as compared to time and eternity. I'd like to remind you of our purpose for being in the world and what it is that God counts as success. Jesus told a story of a small barn and a big fool. A rich man, probably a good man, made one mistake—he left God out of his reckoning and thinking—and his most important question was, "Where am I going to get space to place my goods?"

Finally he concluded, "I need to tear down my small barn and build bigger ones." And as he accumulated much in terms of material possessions, he planned to sit back someday and say, "Eat, drink, and take your ease."

But God, giving us a little insight into this type of person's heart, showed that the great missing link in this man's life was reckoning his Creator in the picture. He forgot that **God** was keeping his heart beating, that **God** — the very author of life!— was responsible for the blood flowing through his veins. This man had become so self-sufficient that he believed himself responsible for keeping things going.

Now, I believe that God is keeping my heart beating at this very moment. No scientist in the world can produce the wonders that make up the human body. In fact, there is not a man today who can create a kernel of corn from nothing, let

6

Like the man who tore down his barns to build larger ones, we frequently forget God in our reckoning, trying to build our security around "things."

alone a human body! Oh, I've seen some kernels of corn that have looked pretty good, but after they're planted in the ground, you could water them until Doomsday, and they'll never grow! Scientists can analyze a kernel of corn and tell you exactly what ingredients are in it and in what proportions; they can even assemble these together, but there's still something missing—life! And the greatest scientist cannot produce one kernel of corn that will produce hundreds more kernels of corn.

Some people believe that God started life on this earth and then let it automatically continue thereafter, but I believe that the great God of the universe is keeping my heart beating moment by moment, right now! And this same God invites us to consider life in terms of how He values success. Yet in our world, everything is viewed according to man-made standards. We usually measure success by material possessions—that's the human thing to do—and when we see someone who has succeeded materially in the world, we admire him.

I once read a list of successful men who had amassed giant fortunes. Two were tied for first place with a billion and a half dollars apiece: Howard Hughes and J. Paul Getty. Now, I don't have any burden to be where Howard Hughes is, and I'm not so sure I want to trade places with J. Paul Getty, either. But it is interesting to note that their wealth was still short of one of the wealthiest men whose name is still around—John D. Rockefeller. When Rockefeller died, he was worth two billion dollars!

One day I tried to figure out how long it would take me to accumulate that much money. I figured that if I could put $2,000 in the bank at the end of the year, I'd be happy. (That's almost $2,000 **more** than I put in each year!) If I could do that at the end of every year, how long would it take me to have as much money as Rockefeller had when he died? It would take a **million years.** That's a lot of money! Yet when the New York papers announced Rockefeller's death, the headlines said, "John D. Pays His Last Debt." And the millions I might accumulate in this world are worthless when it comes to prolonging life. Andrew Carnegie once said that he would give his doctor a million dollars for every year that he kept him alive after the age of 80. But money does not buy life!

Life must have some greater purpose than financial success, and the Bible clearly states what this purpose is. John 3:16 tells us there are only two ways: "For God so loved the world, that He gave His only begotten Son, that whosoever believeth in Him **should not perish**, but **have everlasting life**." Just two ways: perish or live forever. Matthew 7:13, 14 describes these as the broad way, which many choose, and the narrow way, which few can find. Why? Because it's too hard to find? No, people overlook the plan of salvation becaue it's so simple, and they're not interested in it. Most want to do it **their** way. if you were to ask many people about their concept of God, salvation, and how to reach His kingdom, you would find again and again the answer, "Oh, you have to live by the Golden Rule."

Now, I believe in the Golden Rule; I think it is a wonderful rule, **but it is not enough!** A person can take a surface glance at the

8

**My very existence is dependent on God's
continual efforts on my behalf; it is by
His power that my heart continues to beat.**

Golden Rule and still leave God completely out of the picture.
**But salvation and eternal life have to do with a direct con-
frontation with the great God of the universe as revealed in
Jesus Christ.** That's where it's all at! And so Jesus made it clear
that we have a choice to go one of two ways: eternal life or
death, and it has to do with accepting the story of the great
plan of salvation and the Cross.

One day I walked into the intensive care unit of a hospital to
visit someone who had tried to commit suicide. This lady had
been very discouraged, and she just about succeeded with
her wish to die. I stood by her bedside as she came from
underneath that deep sleep, and I'll never forget her anger
when she realized that she still had to face life. She exclaimed,

"I had no choice coming into this world! So I ought to be able to have a choice going out!"

Well, now, that makes sense. None of us had a choice coming into this world! Then whose responsibility was it?

"Well," you say, "my father and mother are responsible."

No. Who is the **author** of life? It's still **God**!

Who is responsible for my being born? God is. Who is responsible for my being born in a world of sin? God still is! He is not responsible for this world of sin, but He **is** responsible for my being here.

If He is responsible for my birth, then He is also responsible for me concerning the options that I must face sometime during my life. Has God ever held us responsible for being born sinners? No! If I am not responsible for having been born in a world of sin, then my only concern is my rejection or acceptance of the plan of salvation that God has provided to answer the sin problem. And it's very evident that God is extremely patient with me while I'm trying to understand it.

God understands our dilemma, and He sent Jesus here as a real person. He knows what it's like to walk around in a world that suffers from the results of sin—the pain, tiredness, and anxiety. And He knows what tears are like. But Jesus always kept in mind the total picture of His mission, and His life is our example of how to live.

Once we grasp the vision of the **privilege** of being born in this world in the light of the opportunity for life eternal, and as we continue to think clearly concerning the issues of time and eternity, it seems that nothing in the world will keep us from accepting God's great plan.

The Bible tells us that "the days of our years are three-score years and ten (70); and if by reason of strength they be fourscore years (80), yet is their strength labour and sorrow; for it is soon cut off"—Psalm 90:10. Even if I live to be 80 or 100, my strength is still labor and sorrow!

One time my father said to me, "Son, I have a proposition to make."

I said, "O.K. What is it?"

"I want you to pretend that I'm a multimillionaire who's going to give you a million dollars. But there are two conditions. First, you have to spend the million dollars all in one year."

Would you be interested? That doesn't sound very difficult,

Life is busy; but we must avoid losing our perspective, getting so involved with "details" that we "can't see the forest for the trees."

does it?

My father continued, "I don't care how you spend it. You can go anywhere in the world; you can buy anything you want, travel, live in luxury. The second condition, however, is that at the end of the year, you die in the gas chamber."

When I heard the second condition, I began to do some fancy thinking. I figured that if I had a million dollars, my father would never catch me! But he said, "No, there's no way out. That's it. You'd have only one year to live. Are you interested?"

I said, "No, thanks!"

"Why not?"

"Because I'd be thinking about the gas chamber all year!" And where I had been looking at the trees, I suddenly saw the forest looming up!

My father transferred his proposition to things of eternity. He asked, "Would you like to live for 70 years just as you want to? No rules or regulations. You can do anything or go anywhere for 70 years. But at the end of this time, you'll end up in the same place prepared for the devil and his angels."

You know, there's an intelligent being who was so smart, he ruined his life. And now he offers this same proposition to each of us: "Look, I've got a deal to make. I'll give you 70 years in which you can do as you please, but at the end of the 70 years, you'll come and burn with me in the lake of fire."

And though he doesn't even have the 70 years to give, millions of people have accepted his proposition!

So when it comes to thinking about life, time, and eternity, I'd like to invite you to use logic and reason. In mathematics I learned that:

$$\frac{2}{4} = \frac{4}{8}$$

There is nothing too profound about that, but I knew that it was in proportion, for when I cross-multiplied, one side equaled the other:

$$2x8 = 16 \text{ and } 4x4 = 16$$

Now, if I transfer the idea of proportions to life and eternity:

$$\frac{1}{70} = \frac{70}{E(\text{eternity})}$$

Is **this** in balance?

$$70x70 = 4,900 \text{ and } 1xE = 1E$$

Is 4,900 equal to eternity? No. This equation is not in balance because of the "E"!

Then, if it is stupid to take the one year and die, when I have 70 to live, isn't it just as stupid, or even more stupid, to take 70 years and die, rather than to have life for eternity? Is that reasonable? But while it is the wise thing to accept God's great plan of salvation, we don't always think that clearly on the subject.

All too often, the questions that occupy our minds soar no higher than the very mundane facets of life.

One time I gave a commencement address to a group of students who were graduating into the first grade. It was kindergarten graduation, and it was a real responsibility to be the speaker for that kind of situation! The pressure was horrible just trying to keep their attention, let alone **say** anything! And you don't get up in front of those kids and tell them about the innate propulsion of the animal kingdom, animated by the supreme activity of the subconscious mind, and superinduced by posterior spheres of the cerebral afterglow! You don't do that kind of thing! I wondered what to do. There they sat, wearing their little crepe-paper robes and their cardboard mortarboards with little tassels hanging down, and I was supposed to give their commencement address.

**Of what value would be all the attractions
of this brief world if on the doorstep of
eternity I found myself outside God's city?**

The only solution I could think of was to get them involved in the program. So I said to them, "Let's pretend that in my right hand I have a note for a million dollars. If you choose this hand, you can cash in on it when you're 21. In my left hand, I have a dime which you can have right now if you choose it. Now, I want you to decide which hand to choose. Be careful! I want you to think clearly and reason this out. I'll give you some time to think."

As I watched the little wheels begin to turn around in their heads, I could see popsicles going by. I could see bubble gum and all sorts of other goodies that a dime would buy. And I cautioned them, "Wait, now, think carefully. Don't be in a hurry!"

I could see their eyes getting bigger and bigger, and I was nervous, because I had tried this once before, with disastrous

Trying to live a complete life without God is like trying to lift a great weight with a chain that has a weak link.

results. So I continued to impress upon them that they must think carefully of their options: a million dollars in the future, or a dime right now?

After I figured they had been given plenty of time, I said, "All right, now, which do you choose?" And they **all** chose . . . the **dime**! I could tell by the pleased looks on their faces that they **knew** I would be happy with their **wise** choice. They were thinking like graduates—going into the first grade!

Later I tried this same experiment with a group of teenagers. One of the young fellows in the back of the room said, "A dime? Oh, c'mon, now! You've got to raise the ante a little bit more!"

"All right," I agreed, "we'll make it a sports car of your choice. If you choose that, you can have it right now, or you can have the million dollars when you're 21. Which do you choose?"

I'd already told them about the graduation from kiddie campus; so they knew the answer they were supposed to give. And this young fellow reasoned, "If I did choose the sports car, it would probably be out in the wrecking yard by the time I was 21. I'd better take the million dollars."

We live in a "now" generation which says, "The things I like to do, I like to do **right now!**" Is this kind of reasoning confined only to the little kids and the young people? No, it's one of the easiest things in the world to think purely in terms of the moment and to forget about tomorrow. And suddenly the forest gets lost through the trees.

My father gave me this project, and I've pursued it since. One of his favorite questions is to ask people if they'd like to live life over again.

"Oh, yes!" they'd say. "I sure would. I'd do a lot of things differently."

No, that isn't the question. Would you like to live life over again if you could live it exactly as you have already lived it? No changes; all the joys, all the sorrows. Would you?

Inevitably the older a person is and the more he has seen of life, the quicker he responds, "No!" A young person who hasn't seen much may choose to relive his life, but when he begins to get together the total span of life, just thinking of it from a worldly sense without Christ in the picture, he usually says, "No!"

If life, as far as this world is concerned, is not worth living over again, then may I propose to you without fear of contradiction that the greatest challenge facing us is to accept God's plan and prepare for eternal life. Is that fair enough? There is no question more important than that.

Then what is the most important question of all the important questions? Mark 8:36: "**What shall it profit a man, if he shall gain the whole world, and lose his own soul**?" I grew up seeing this text on a sign at the back of the auditoriums where my father and uncle held evangelistic meetings. Before I started playing in the sawdust, making airplanes, I'd go through a little ritual: I'd look at those big bold letters of that sign—the letters still burn into my vision today—and follow the lines of every letter: "W-H-A-T S-H-A-L-L I-T P-R-O-F-I-T A M-A-N .... What shall it profit a man, if he shall gain the whole world, and lose his own soul? Mark 8:36." I'll never forget it!

There is no question but that there can be "fun" in a life without God; the problem is that the "fun" doesn't last!

That is the most important question facing all of us right now. There is nothing more important! And as we consider the options, we are inevitably led to decide, "All right, what shall I do about it?" If I were to amass two billion dollars, but end up outside the gates of the city of God someday, then it would have been better if I had never been born.

"Well," someone says, "I'm not sure about the 'E'. Is there an eternity?"

All right. Just for the sake of logic, without taking the Bible into it, I'll give you a 50-50 chance that there is no eternity, if you'll grant me a 50-50 chance that there is. If there is no eternity, then at the end of this life, both you and I will go to the same dust, we'll remain there a long time, and neither one of us will have anything over the other. But if there is an eternity, you have missed **everything.**

"Oh," you say, "think of all the fun, the excitement, and adventure you can have if you don't have any rules and regulations!"

I remember an occasion, early in my life, when the carnival with its whirligigs and sideshows came to town, and everyone else was going. My brother and I knew what our dad would say, but we asked him anyway if we could go.

To our surprise he replied, "I think it's time you made your own decisions. You know how I feel about things like that, but I'm going to leave it up to you."

"Really? You're going to let us decide?"

"Yes."

So we went to the carnival. The first half was tremendous! Lots of fun! We spent our money like water. Tried everything. Then we began to get dizzy, sort of sick to our stomachs. And as we left the carnival that night, knowing that father was home praying for us, we had discovered that it was fun while it lasted, but it didn't last!

Down with the person who says there is no fun in the world! There **is** fun, **but it doesn't last**. I believe that most everyone is searching continually for things to create fun, to replace that vacuum within, when the fun goes away. People running here and there, looking for something to satisfy the longing, always searching for something better and lasting.

If the lasting solution to our restlessness is the plan of salvation, then the question comes, "What am I going to do with Jesus Christ who has made it all possible?" What am I going to do with Jesus?

Now, every once in a while, someone says, "I don't need God. I'm getting along without Him." I'd like to suggest something else to you. The question is not so much whether or not I need God, but whether or not God needs me. Does God need **me**?

II Corinthians 8:9 describes the sacrifice of Christ: "For ye know the grace of our Lord Jesus Christ, that, though He was rich, yet for your sakes He became poor, that ye through His poverty might be rich." There's something beautiful about that text. If He became poor for my sake, then the least I could do is to accept His riches for His sake. I don't need God? But God needs me! If He had enough interest to create me and redeem me with His life, then I ought to be interested in Him for **His** sake.

**Getting acquainted with God by spending time alone
with Him each day is the most significant thing
I can do with the time allotted to me.**

Therefore, studying God's Word, accepting His grace, getting acquainted with Him, and daily spending quiet time alone continuing in His love and His plan of salvation is the most significant thing I could do with the time allotted me.

I'm thankful that Jesus invites us to "come now and reason together,"—to use our heads and think. Psalm 90:12 says, "So teach us to number our days, that we may apply our hearts unto wisdom."

Dear Father in Heaven, thank You for Jesus and His great mission of love. We don't deserve it; we haven't done anything to merit it, but our hearts are humbled in awe and gratitude. We realize that You have created and redeemed us—that You want us—and we pray that You will help us to place everything else of secondary consideration aside and to face in the light of the cross the great claims of Heaven. We thank You for inviting us to learn to know You, and that while we are learning, we can have the assurance that though our sins are as scarlet, they shall be as white as snow. We respond to Your love, in Jesus' name, Amen.

2

The Good Fight
of Faith

The community desperately needed rain. The wells were dry and the crops were parched. So the preacher called a special prayer meeting. The church was packed that night. One little girl even brought her umbrella!

The congregation smiled at the child's demonstration of faith. But when the rain came a few minutes later, the little girl was the only one who didn't get wet.

What caused the rain? Was it the little girl and her umbrella? Or did she bring the umbrella because she **knew** it was going to rain. Your interpretation of the story will probably depend on your understanding of faith and how it operates.

There are many people who think that faith is simply positive thinking—that if you can make yourself believe strongly enough that something is going to happen, it **will** happen. These people think of faith as something that is self-generated, something to work up. One of the most common understandings of faith in Christian circles is that "faith is believing." Other common definitions are that "faith is taking God at His Word," or "faith is believing what God says." These concepts of faith are insufficient and intangible. No wonder we are told that the earth is almost destitute of true faith (Luke 18:8)—we scarcely know what true faith really is.

Let's consider a Bible experience, found in Matthew 15:21-28 **(Today's English Version)**, where Jesus commended a woman for her faith, and see how these definitions fit.

"Jesus left that place and went off to the territory near the cities of Tyre and Sidon. A Canaanite woman who lived in that region came to him. 'Son of David!' she cried out. 'Have mercy on me! My daughter has a demon and is in a terrible condition.' But Jesus did not say a word to her."

It was not uncommon for the Jews to ignore the Canaanites. But it is never pleasant to be ignored. It would seem that this woman would have given up and gone away. But she didn't.

"His disciples came to him and begged him, 'Send her away! She is following us and making all this noise!'" And Jesus apparently agreed with them, for He replied, "I have been sent only to those lost sheep, the people of Israel." He might as well have said, "I didn't come to help **her**."

"At this the woman came and fell at his feet. 'Help me, sir!' she said."

And Jesus answered, "It isn't right to take the children's food and throw it to the dogs."

Have you ever been ignored when you asked for help, and then, when you persisted in your request, been insulted? Have you ever been called a dog? It seems surprising that this woman didn't give up long before Jesus got to the "dogs" part. But she found the opening she had been looking for. Jesus must have had a twinkle in His eye during the whole conversation. And the Canaanite woman must have seen it. Because she answered, "That's true, sir, but even the dogs eat the leftovers that fall from their masters' table." In other words, if I am a dog, then at least I'm entitled to some dog food!

Then Jesus answered her, "You are a woman of great faith! What you want will be done for you." And at that very moment her daughter was healed.

Now let me ask you: How is faith defined in this story? Is it taking God at His word? No, if the woman had taken God at His word, she would have given up. Do you define faith in terms of believing, or believing what God says? You can't; it doesn't fit. Faith in her case was **dis**believing what Jesus said. Faith was **not** taking Him at His word.

Because of inadequate definitions of faith, there has developed a very subtle form of pseudo-faith. I remember listening to a record entitled "How to Become a Success." The speaker, 35 years of age, had retired on an income of $35,000

**Unlike the interpretation some give
to the story of the little girl and her umbrella,
faith is not a means of making things happen
because we believe strongly enough.**

a year. His theme was that you must believe in yourself and your marvelous mind in order to be a success. He quoted a few Bible texts to support his view and proposed that the only barrier to success was the failure to believe in one's own abilities. If his listeners would try his plan for 30 days, he promised, they would be successful in anything they wanted to do. His logic almost made sense, but I couldn't help remembering a Bible text that said, "He that trusteth in his own heart (or mind) is a fool"—Proverbs 28:26.

The common denominator of counterfeit faith, regardless of what form it takes, is the idea that you can make yourself believe something; and that if you believe hard enough, this will cause God to move. It boils down to a type of mental gymnastics, or positive thinking, and perhaps its greatest danger is that it inevitably becomes self-centered, just as working hard on trying to overcome your sins makes you become self-centered.

With a false faith, a person's concept of God, and of understanding God's will, becomes confused. Some Christians believe that if you have enough faith, any promise you can find in God's Word is immediately His will. This kind of person will work hard to make himself believe that certain promises are going to be fulfilled in his case, or in someone else's case, and he hinges his confidence and love for God on whether or not he gets adequate answers. He will often take scriptures out of context, and he begins to use God as a sort of Santa Claus or Aladdin's lamp. His primary purpose in prayer is to get answers.

The tragic thing is that a strong-minded person might be able to succeed in this to a certain extent, and he finds himself believing or having faith in **himself**, not God. And because he seems to have success, his self-generated faith can become a deadly escape from the personal relationship with Christ. He sees no need of God. That is why positive thinking is not faith. It has never been faith and never will be faith! Instead, it is a subtle form of "salvation by my own works," a "glory trip" in which I take the credit for having enough genius to cause things to happen. And when I do not succeed in getting the answers I want, my spiritual life can be devastated.

A man burst into my office one day and said, "You can have your God, and your faith, and your religion, and your Bible. I'm through with the whole business."

"Why? What's the matter?"

"My wife just died. And I have read in Scripture that 'Whatsoever you ask in prayer, believing, you shall receive.' For two years I believed that my wife wouldn't die. I told her every day, 'Don't worry, you're not going to die.' And now she's dead. And I'm through with God. Forget it."

This man didn't make any bones about it. He didn't blame himself—he felt his faith had been absolute. It was **God** who had failed!

Did this man have faith? No—he didn't know the first thing about faith. His reactions in the time of crisis proved it.

The first year I was in the ministry someone called me to the bedside of a dying man. The relatives and friends wanted us to

**"I believe, I believe"—too often people
understand faith as something self-generated,
for which we get credit in Heaven.**

pray and annoint him. I thought at that time that if a person
could believe strongly enough—that if they could take the
courage of Peter and John at the Gate Beautiful, and could say,
"In the name of Jesus, rise up"—that it would happen. And that
God wouldn't act unless someone did that.

Well, I went to the man's bedside. We annointed him with oil,
and prayed. When we opened our eyes after the prayer, I
looked around to see who would have the courage of Peter
and John. But everyone was looking at me! And I didn't have
the courage. I quickly thought up some rationalizations, and
mumbled something about God answering prayer in different
ways, sometimes right away, and sometimes not until later, and
I beat a hasty retreat. The man died, and I thought I killed him
because I didn't believe strongly enough.

25

You don't go through that type of experience more than once without getting down to the study of exactly what this business of faith is all about.

The Bible makes it clear that everyone is given enough faith to get started. Romans 12:3 says, "God has given to every man the measure of faith." Usually we think of faith in terms of **quantity**. Therefore we try to increase the amount we have. Jesus' disciples had the same idea, and one day they asked Jesus to increase their faith (Luke 17).

Jesus replied, "If your faith were even as much as the amount of a grain of mustard seed, you could move mountains."

What was He saying? He was saying that it wasn't the amount of faith that was so important; it was whether or not they had **genuine** faith. God looks at our faith in terms of **quality**, not **quantity**. If we had the real thing, then just the amount of a grain of mustard seed could work wonders.

Yet faith **does** grow as it is exercised. Have you ever wondered how to exercise faith? Is faith exercised by putting yourself in difficult places, and then expecting God to bail you out? Is faith exercised by writing checks when your bank balance is zero, and then waiting for God to cover the checks? Do you exercise faith by claiming promises?

I recently met a family that had decided they should move to the country. They bought a piece of land, and were ready to build their house, but there was no water on the land.

Then someone came to town to teach people how to claim promises. The family asked him to come out and help them claim a promise, and they gathered out at the farm. They claimed the promise, "Seek and ye shall find"—which, by the way, has nothing whatever to do with finding water in a well.

But water came! The family rejoiced, built their house, and moved to the new location. Then the well went dry. When I last saw them, they were very confused people. Was there something wrong with their faith? Was there something wrong with the promise? Or was there something wrong with God?

A student was coming back to college after vacation. He was on a plane with a faculty member, and because of a dense fog, they couldn't land at the airport as planned. The student said to the faculty member beside him, "Watch this! I'm

**When Jesus talked about faith and moving mountains
He was revealing that what matters
is not quantity but quality of faith.**

going to claim a promise, and the fog will go away."

He did claim a promise, but the fog didn't go away. And that was one discouraged student.

What he didn't realize was that it might not be necessary for him to land at that particular airport. Perhaps God's will was for him to land at some other location. In fact, there have been good people, godly people, who have gone down in plane crashes—and it was neither because they were lacking in faith, nor because they didn't know how to claim the right promise.

Two men were burned at the stake. Their names were Huss and Jerome. And they are only two of thousands who perished during the Dark Ages. If claiming promises is the right method to get God to act, then Huss and Jerome really missed it. For

27

there is a beautiful promise in Isaiah 43:2 that says, "When thou passest through the waters, I will be with thee; and through the rivers, they shall not overflow thee; when thou walkest through the fire, thou shalt not be burned; neither shall the flame kindle upon thee."

But don't tell me that Huss and Jerome died because they didn't have the right kind of faith. If I understand it correctly, Huss and Jerome died because they **did** have faith. And part of the promise was fulfilled for them, even without their claiming it, for it says, "When thou walkest through the fire, thou shalt not be burned." Huss and Jerome died singing! Have you ever put your hand on a hot stove? Did you sing? Nobody dies at the stake with green wood and a slow fire—**singing**—unless they are not being burned. But the last half of that scripture, "neither shall the flame kindle upon thee," was not fulfilled. The singing martyrs were reduced to ashes, and their ashes were thrown in the river.

John the Baptist was beheaded. Elisha died after a long, lingering illness—Elisha, who had been given a double portion of Elijah's spirit. And "these all died in faith"—which tells us that faith is something far more than making yourself believe that God will answer prayer in the way you have detailed it.

I do not believe that every promise you can find in God's Word is God's will for you, at this time, and under these circumstances. John the Baptist, and Elisha, and Huss and Jerome, and a host of others, have proved that.

There are some promises in God's Word, however, that **are** always God's will. Those are the promises that have to do with spiritual blessings. It is **always** God's will to forgive us from sin, to give us His grace and power, to give us wisdom to do His work. These promises we may claim. For these blessings we are to ask, and believe that we receive, and return thanks that we have received. But it is obvious from the lives of godly people that when it comes to temporal blessings, including life and health, that unless a person knows by special revelation what God's will is on a subject, he must pray, "Thy will be done."

What is genuine faith, then? It is more than taking God at His word. It's more than making yourself believe. Genuine faith is never worked at, it is never worked up. When you study it, you come to the only definition of faith that will fit. It's just one word. **Trust**. Genuine faith is trusting God.

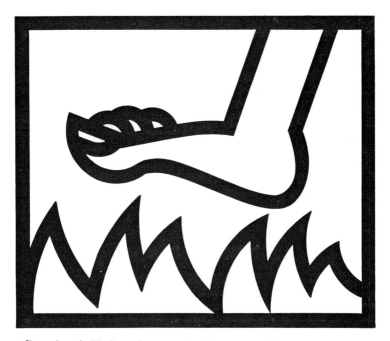

Genuine faith is not a magic show or an insurance policy protecting us from the flames and trials of life; it is trusting God in the midst of life's challenges.

The Greek word from which "faith" is translated in the New Testament is also translated in at least two other ways—"belief" and "trust." All come from the same Greek word. Therefore, you can take "belief" or "faith," whenever you find them, and without damaging the thought or the context, substitute the word "trust." For instance, "This is the victory that overcometh the world, even our faith" (I John 5:4) can be changed to "This is the victory that overcometh the world, even our **trust**." Acts 16:31, "Believe in the Lord Jesus Christ and thou shalt be saved," can read, "**Trust** in the Lord Jesus Christ . . . ." I Timothy 6:12, "Fight the good fight of **trust**."

This is **not** the same as merely saying, "I believe." In our world today there is a cheap kind of faith which only demands that you "believe in Christ" in order to be saved. No!

29

Learning to **trust** God requires something deeper than that—it demands a personal, continuing **relationship** with a God who is completely trustworthy.

What is the genuine fight of faith? What is our part? Jesus said that our work is to **trust** (John 6:28). We fight the good fight of learning to **trust**! That involves getting to know one who is trustworthy.

Unfortunately, most of us immediately confuse the good fight of faith, or trust, with the bad fight of sin. We think that fighting the good fight of faith consists of trying hard to live a good life. The problem is that the strong person who fights sin might outwardly succeed to some degree, but becomes proud of his success, and also fails to see his need of God. On the other hand, the weak person who tries to change his life by fighting sin doesn't even outwardly succeed—and he becomes discouraged. Neither understands what the fight of faith is all about.

When I was a pastor in Oregon, I was asked to visit a married couple who were backsliders. They were mad at preachers and vowed that the next preacher who came along would be tossed out in the dust.

When I went to their home, they kindly invited me inside and, much to my surprise, said, "We're backsliders."

Then they laughed. It was a laugh I'll never forget, because it was a laugh of nervousness, but also of relief.

As we visited, it soon became apparent that they had backslidden from the idea that religion consisted of don'ts. If it tasted good, they shouldn't eat it; if it looked good, they shouldn't watch it; if it sounded good, they shouldn't listen to it; and if it was fun, they shouldn't do it!

They were fighting the bad fight of sin, and in the process, they found religion to be toilsome, difficult, and gloomy. All of their efforts to keep the law were to no avail. They should have been fighting the good fight of faith instead. Once they understood that the power for victory comes only from knowing Jesus Christ, they became excited about religion again.

The truth is that you don't have to do bad things to be a sinner, and not doing bad things does not make you a Christian. In order to be a sinner, all you have to do is to be born, because all of us are born with inherent sinful natures. The Bible tells us that all unrighteousness is sin (1 John 5:17), and that "there is none righteous, no, not one," because "**all** have sinned"

**If you want to have apples, you get an apple tree;
in the same way, if you want faith, you don't work at
faith, you must get to the cause of faith.**

(Romans 3:10, 23). While some are better able to keep from doing bad things, they are actually no better off than the weak
people who are obviously suffering defeat in their Christian experience.

So where should we direct our efforts in order to get genuine
faith, or trust? Some people think we should work on trying to
produce the faith—but I'd like to remind you that an apple tree
bears apples because **it is an apple tree**, never **in order to
become an apple tree**. If you want to have apples, then you
get an apple tree. If you want genuine faith, pay attention to
the cause of faith.

Of course, that's a simplistic approach, but it's nonetheless
true. There's no point in trying to produce apples apart from an
apple tree. The wax or plastic imitations might appear very

convincing from the outside, but they certainly taste nothing like the real apples from an apple tree!

I remember being in kindergarten when we'd celebrate birthdays by bringing out a replica of a cake and singing "Happy Birthday." But we never cut the cake! Now, I'll admit that some of those cakes looked pretty bad—plaster of Paris dripping off one side, and drops of wax from 10 years of use on the other. Some of them, however, looked good enough to eat, and I remember the disappointment that came into my heart and mind when school ended without our ever cutting the cake.

An imitation is always disappointing, and an imitation in terms of faith is disappointing in the end, although it might be flattering to the ego in the beginning.

If I want faith, I don't work on trying to produce faith. Why not? A genuine Christian has faith **because** he knows Jesus. Genuine faith cannot be self-generated; it comes only as the spontaneous result of fellowship with God.

There are at least two conditions to being able to trust anyone. First, you must find someone who is absolutely trustworthy. And second, you must get to know that person. Because a person can be ever so trustworthy, but if you don't **know** him, you won't **trust** him.

It works in the opposite way as well. A person can be absolutely **un**trustworthy, and you won't distrust him until you get to know him. But if you get to know him, you'll automatically distrust him!

You may have heard about the man who put his boy up on a ladder, and told him to jump. The boy jumped, and the man stepped back and let him fall on his face. Then he said, "There. That will teach you never to trust anybody." That's the kind of world we live in. In the early days of our country, according to legends, everyone was trusted until he proved to be untrustworthy. If you owed someone some money, you'd put it in an envelope, and leave it fastened to your front gate. You could go on vacation knowing that no one would touch it except the person it was meant for. Even if he came by a week or so later, he'd find his money still there. But today we live in an age when everyone tends to distrust until someone proves he can be trusted.

An imitation of faith, like a plaster cake, is always unsatisfying, regardless of how colorful and spectacular it may appear to be.

The Bible truth is that God is absolutely trustworthy. Although that's the truth about God, some people don't believe it. And the only reason they don't believe it is because they don't **know** Him. Anyone who is looking over his glasses at God is advertising the fact that he doesn't know Him. Because to know God is to trust Him.

If you get to know someone who is absolutely trustworthy, you will automatically, spontaneously trust him. You won't have to work at it—it will happen naturally. Trust in God is the first thing that happens when we get to know Him, and we don't have to work at it. Genuine faith trusts in God no matter what happens. Faith is trusting God when tragedy strikes, as well as when things are going smoothly. Genuine faith trusts God whether the airplane goes down, whether the well goes dry, in life, or in death. And this "rice-Christian" idea—basing faith on whether or not I get answers to my prayers in the way I expect—is the devil's counterfeit of faith.

Genuine faith is not an end in itself. It does not come to those who seek for it, but to those who seek it not and who seek only Jesus. Faith always has an object. But when faith itself becomes the object, it will destroy us.

Genuine faith can come only as a result of knowing God on a one-to-one, person-to-person basis. And how is this accomplished? In the same way you get to know anyone—by communication. We communicate with others by talking to them, by listening to them talk to us, and by going places and doing things together. In the Christian life, I can talk to God in prayer. I can listen to Him by reading His Word. And I can go places and do things with Him by becoming involved in service and outreach.

The methods of becoming acquainted with God are the elements of a vital devotional life. And when I am in a meaningful relationship with God, day by day, I learn to trust Him—automatically, spontaneously, naturally. This is faith—trust—in its highest sense.

Faith, or trust, is a gift from God. Ephesians 2:8, 9 says, "For by grace are ye saved through faith; and **that** not of yourselves: It is the gift of God." There is only one way to receive a gift, and that is to come into the presence of the giver of the gift. How do you come into God's presence to receive this gift of trust from Him? On your knees before His open Word.

The primary purpose of prayer is friendship and acquaintance with God—not to get answers. And the primary purpose of the Christian witness is to tell about the love of God—not to recount a list of all the answers you have received.

What is the good fight of faith? It is taking the measure of faith already given (Romans 12:3), and using it toward becoming personally acquainted with God each day, learning to know Jesus, so that I can trust Him as a spontaneous result of knowing Him. I never fight for faith—I fight to learn to know God. And it does require effort to maintain that daily acquaintance with God, because the devil knows that you'll receive the power of God unto salvation if you learn to know God (I John 5:4). So Satan does everything he can to distract you and keep you from spending time with God.

My appeal to you, my friend, is that you become engaged in the effort that is involved in knowing God personally. As you become acquainted with Him, you'll receive His gift of faith as a spontaneous result.

What a wonderful privilege to become acquainted with the great God of the universe, to learn to know a God who can be trusted because He is trustworthy! I invite you to begin today to know Him as your personal Friend.

Dear Father in Heaven, thank You for the good news that the life of the Christian is this simple. Forgive us for all of the devious methods, maneuvers, and gimmicks that we've used in trying to get genuine faith. Please deliver us from relying on anything else except Your grace and power, and teach us to know You on a one-to-one basis, so that the genuine faith of Jesus will come into our lives. We thank You for hearing our plea, in Jesus' name, Amen.

3

How to Find Christ

Have you ever wondered if God is lost? In the past, He has seemed to be so lost that some people have even believed Him to be dead. If God isn't lost, then why is it so difficult to find Him?

Several years ago I read a letter written by a college-age young person, and I've never been able to forget the cry for help:

Many of us faithful young church members are in a desperate situation. We have a great, wide, deep need that is not being met. We're starving because we're not being fed.

Please take me seriously, because I know what I'm talking about. Young people are leaving the church every day, bitter, disillusioned, and without hope, while others won't even consider having anything to do with religion, because they see nothing in it to help them.

We don't need more sermons about witnessing to others. We've been told repeatedly to share the gospel, but upon responding to this challenge, we've discovered that we have nothing to say. How can we convince others to look forward to the return of Christ when the majority of us wouldn't even recognize Him if He did come?

We need someone to tell **us** about God. We know all about church doctrines and practices. We know a lot of things, **but we do not know Christ**. We were never

37

introduced to Him, and unless God performs a miracle and reveals Himself to us, we'll never know Him.

Please teach us how to know God and His character. We're spiritual babes. We need Jesus. We're longing to know Him. Show us from your own personal experience how to communicate with Him. Our greatest need is to know God. Can you show us how to find Him?

This question of "how to find Christ" is not just confined to young people 20 years of age. People who have been faithful church members for 20 years have also admitted to the frustration of trying to find Him. Someone once described his despair this way, "I guess God doesn't even know my address."

It's interesting to notice that Bible characters seem to have had the same difficulty trying to find God. Job 23:3 echoes the despairing cry of a hungry soul: "Oh, that I knew where I might find Him." Amos 8:12 speaks of a group of people rushing from sea to sea, coast to coast, looking for the word of the Lord and not being able to find it.

Doesn't this sound discouraging to you? One wonders if it is possible to find God. Is it even possible for man to **initiate** this search for God?

The Bible indicates that some do succeed in their search. There are a few. Matthew 7:14 describes two ways leading to our ultimate destiny. Although the majority of us take the broad way which leads to death, a few manage to find the narrow way which leads to life. Jesus says that if we seek, we will find rest unto our souls (Matthew 7:7; 11:29), and God promises that when we seek Him with all our hearts, we'll find Him (Jeremiah 29:13), for He is never far from us (Acts 17:27).

Evidently, then, there is support for seeking God. We don't have to wait for the right speaker to come along or for the clergy to convince us that we need God. Others may be a help in leading us to know God, but the truth is that God is wherever we are, seeking to draw us to Him, even before we spend much time and energy looking for Him.

I'm reminded of the stories Jesus told about a lost sheep, a lost coin, and a lost son (Luke 15). The tax collectors and other "sinners" were crowding around Him, eagerly listening to His words. On the outskirts of the multitude, the self-righteous Pharisees and doctors of the law began grumbling among
38

**After all our attempts to find God have failed,
and we begin to wonder if He can be found,
we must come to realize
that there is something wrong with our searching.**

themselves, saying, "This man welcomes sinners and even eats with them."

Jesus answered with a parable which demonstrated the great truth that God is out looking for us, and that His efforts surpass our attempts to find Him. And there is encouragement in this threefold parable, for it describes more than the actions of a God who seeks man. It also tells us the kind of people for whom He is searching.

In the first story, a shepherd with a hundred sheep in his fold noticed that one was missing. Somewhere out in the wilderness, the sheep was lost, and if left helpless and alone, it would continue to wander until it died. Even if it realized its plight, it didn't know the way back. Immediately the shepherd went out into the wilderness and searched until he found it.

With great delight he carried it home and called his friends and neighbors together, saying, "Rejoice with me! I've found my lost sheep."

Jesus made it clear that salvation does not come through our seeking after God, but from our response to God's seeking after us. Just like the sheep, we may know that we are lost while not knowing the way back. But God goes out looking for us.

Jesus' second story was about a woman who had 10 silver coins. One night when she counted them, she discovered that one was missing, probably lost somewhere in her own house. She took a lamp and went through the house, looking in every corner for her lost coin. Amid all the furniture and rubble of the household, the search continued, for no matter how small that piece of silver was, it was still valuable in her eyes.

Notice that instead of being lost out in the mountains or the wilderness, this coin was lost in the house. The coin didn't even know it was lost. Its owner knew better, however, and searched until it was found. Then she threw a party to celebrate the finding of the coin. Jesus again emphasized the fact that the value of one soul can never be overestimated in the eyes of Heaven.

Then Jesus concluded His message with the parable of the lost son—an ungrateful son who deliberately calculated to be lost. He left with as many riches as he could take with him and departed into a far country. There he **planned** to lose himself, trying to forget his father, trying to escape. For a while he appeared to have a measure of success—he found friends who helped him spend his money freely. But then came the day when he found himself at the end of his own resources. He went through his overcoat, his suitcoat, and his sweater. He went through his vest and his shirt, and finally "when he came to himself" in the pigpen, he remembered all the love his father had given to him. That same power of love was drawing him back, and he said, "I will arise and go home to my father."

Is there forgiveness for deliberate sin? Does God forgive backsliders who **plan** to get lost? This parable indicates that even though we know our way back, God is still out there at the front gate with His binoculars each day, watching for us down the road. When He sees us, He runs out to welcome us back with great rejoicing and happiness.

In the serious or casual search for God, few take the narrow road of self-surrender; most take the broad, easy way that leads only to eternal loss.

In these three illustrations, Jesus demonstrates the goodness and the kindness of the Father. Each of us falls into one of these categories at some point in our lives. We may know we're lost and yet not realize the way back; we may not even know we're lost; or we may deliberately plan to be lost, even though we know the way back. Jesus assures us that God is out looking for all three kinds of people. **All** are valuable, and Heaven rejoices whenever any individuals are saved.

That's God's business. That's what the plan of salvation is all about. God isn't an evasive being who is playing a game of hide-and-seek while our eternal destiny hangs in the balance. He isn't trying to elude us. Instead, we serve a God who never leaves us wandering and alone, whether we know we're lost or not, whether we know the way back or whether we don't.

The reason we can't find God is that we spend most of our time and energy running from Him, attempting to elude facing our greatest need: self-surrender.

God takes the initiative in each case, staying with us, drawing us to Him, and waiting until we realize His presence. We continue to seek Him because He first sought us. We love Him because He first loved us—all the way from a world of glory into a world of sin and trouble. He's always looking for us.

"Well," says someone, "if Christ is looking for us, then why is it so difficult to find Him?"

The problem has always been the same, ever since the very beginning when sin entered our world. We can't find Him because we spend most of our energy and effort in running from Him, and sometimes we run even **after** we've found Him, too.

Adam ran, through the trees and shrubs of the garden of Eden, knowing that God would soon be coming to com-

The mystical ladder Jacob saw was God's assurance of forgiveness, even for deliberate sin, and His steadfast desire to have us enter a living communion with Him.

municate with him, as He did each day. Adam was afraid to face Him after going against His wishes. Finally he found a dense bush and hid behind it, hoping God wouldn't see him. But God came running after him.

Jacob ran from his home and family, out into the desert. His brother was out to kill him, and he figured life was just about over. In exhaustion he lay down on the dusty roadside, put his head on a rock, and tried to sleep. Then he saw the mystical ladder from earth to Heaven. God had been following him, and he was thrilled with the realization that God still loved him despite his treachery.

Jonah fled from God, too. Afraid to carry God's message to Nineveh, he ran away. On a ship out on the high seas, he thought he'd finally succeeded in escaping, but God followed him clear into the belly of the whale.

Saul of Tarsus tried to kill every Christian in Jerusalem. From there he left for Damascus, in a hurry to put an end to the new Christians. God ran after him, willing to forgive the past and ready to help Saul build a new life in Him. He followed along the Damascus road, reminding Saul of a dying man's prayer, "Father, don't hold this sin against them."

It's very hard to get away from God, but often we will try everything we can, every maneuver and escape, trying to outrun Him. And in all cases, we are really running away from the same thing—self-surrender. We're trying to escape that moment of truth in which we are faced with the realization that we are incapable of handling life and the things of eternity. Our pride and ego make it very difficult for us to give up on ourselves. Our humanistic hearts prefer the "do-it-yourself" religion in which we rely on our abilities and inner resources. We want to hang onto something that we can do; so we invent all sorts of ways to escape from self-surrender.

Often we try to keep occupied with enough legitimate concerns such as studies or work so we won't have to think seriously about the issues of time and eternity and relationship with God. College students like to complain about having too much to do and not enough time to do it. But looking back on my own college years, I find them to be the most carefree days of my life, for each year that has gone by brings more duties and responsibilities, while time seems to move faster and faster. Someone gave me a book with the intriguing title of **How to Live on 24 Hours a Day.** I plan to read it someday. I haven't yet, because I don't have enough time!

If we're not trying to escape through the mundane duties of life, then we become absorbed in pleasure. We run from ourselves and from God, always on the go, always looking for one more excitement or thrill to keep us from thinking about the future. Pleasure-oriented escapism. We develop what is called the "antsy" syndrome, a modern term for the eternal fidgets. If we can't find enough business or pleasure to keep us occupied, we go crazy, because the worst torture in the world would be having time in which to think about God and eternity. Although we complain about being overworked, we're happy because it helps to keep us from self-surrender.

One fallacious route to God is sensationalism or emotionalism, where the right combination of hand-clapping or tear-shedding substitutes for self-surrender.

Another escape route is through pseudo-religion. We put on all of the show and externals of religious behavior and vocabulary. We become experts at faking, at acting, at pretending we're close to God when we're not. When we can't accept a personal relationship of dependence on God, we look for ways of avoiding Him that will pass as ways of remembering Him. We like to spend a great deal of time discussing, dissecting, and analyzing religious themes. Usually there is no practical value to such speculations, but they do display our mental gymnastics and fool other people into thinking we're religious.

All along, however, even while we're deliberately trying to run away from God, He is following us, staying close, helping us when we don't know it, guiding us when we don't intend it. He

45

remains with us, looking for the chance to let us know that He loves and cares for us even while we're running away.

There is an even more subtle way to run from God, however, one that we are not always aware of or willing to admit. After we realize our need of God, we may still balk at the idea of self-surrender. So we try to make up our own routes to salvation. **We** take the initiative in the search, thinking ourselves capable of finding Him.

Many of us work on behavioral changes—something tangible to do. We analyze ourselves, trying to seek God through self-realization, using the psychological approach without God as its center and without Christ as foremost. We try to give up our sinful practices and habits, our evil associations, our wickedness. If we manage to succeed in modifying our behavior, if we succeed in being good, moral people, then we think we've found God.

Sometimes we believe we've found God when we have just the right combination of tender feelings and emotional highs. Sensational religion, not grounded on the Word of God. We seek a certain atmosphere and try to be surrounded by the right kind of people. Success in finding God is measured by the number of tears that are shed, the shivers that go up and down our spines, the soft lights and the music that help us feel religious. Somehow we think that if we can just get the right setting, we'll receive enough of a spiritual injection to last until the next great emotional revival somewhere.

And so it goes on, all kinds of escape methods from the moment of truth in which we realize the necessity of surrendering to God. We try to escape by answering an altar call or coming to the church or the pastor. We try to escape by determining never to do certain types of things again. We make all kinds of promises and efforts. But as the days go by, our closets are empty of our kneeprints, and the cover of our Bible in which the life and character of Jesus is portrayed gathers dust on our shelves.

"All right," says someone. "So it's true that we're running away from God. What can we do about it? How do we surrender?"

First of all, we must have a desire for something better than we are presently experiencing. This desire cannot be self-generated; it can only come from God, Christ, and the Holy Spirit. All three work constantly to bring us to this realization.

Spiritual life doesn't come by injection; it comes through communion, daily taking time to study the gospels on the life of Christ and communicate with God.

Next we must gain a knowledge of the plan of salvation. This is something that God will not force us to learn; we have to place ourselves in the environment in which that happens—wherever His Word is read, spoken, or taught. God doesn't try to cram a knowledge of His plan of salvation down our throats. Often religionists run ahead of the Holy Spirit. While He talks in a still, small voice, they're out there clobbering others with two-by-fours until they're driven away from God. But God isn't pushy. He stays with us, never forcing Himself on us, but never abandoning us. When we run, He's right behind us.

The third step in coming to Christ is admitting that we've been running, trying to escape from Him through all sorts of ways. If we take a long look at ourselves, we'll have to recognize our sinful condition. God doesn't operate in a vacuum, and He helps us to face ourselves, not in order to dwell upon our imperfections, but to honestly realize our helplessness and then admit it, without excuses and alibis.

The final step in coming to Christ is the hardest of all, and it is at this point that many of us start running again. We must acknowledge that we have no ability to change ourselves. Although God is running after us, He can't help us until we are at the point of great need. And just like the prodigal son, we don't usually want to come to Jesus until we get to the end of our own resources. As one writer has said, "The Lord can do nothing toward the recovery of man until, convinced of his own weakness, and stripped of all self-sufficiency, he yields himself to the control of God. Then he can receive the gift that God is waiting to bestow. From the soul that feels his need, nothing is withheld"—**The Desire of Ages**, p. 300.

Whenever people try to find Christ without first realizing their great need of Him, without realizing their own resources will not suffice, they always end up frustrated. Some people have to go through unnecessary hardships before they'll admit their need for Christ, just as they don't feel the need for fire insurance until their house is on fire. It's the sense of need that makes the difference, and some never do come to that point of giving up on themselves, which is what surrender is all about.

Have you ever had the impression that God never cared about you? Have you ever felt He didn't even know your address or phone number? Perhaps you haven't yet come to the point of surrender in your own life. You've still been holding on to the idea that you can do something yourself.

We cannot find Christ until we search **with all our heart**, as though it were a life-and-death issue. We can't do that until we've given up on ourselves and on every other resource. When we do realize our need, the only thing we can do is to admit our helplessness and ask God to take over.

How do we get our sense of need? There are two routes, and most of us, unfortunately, take the long route. We keep on running. As C.S. Lewis describes it:

So here, the shock comes at the precise moment when the thrill of **life** is communicated to us along the clue we have been following. It is always shocking to meet life where we thought we were alone. 'Look out!' we cry, 'It's **alive**!' And therefore this is the very point at

Many of us hide, self-satisfied, behind a benign view of God, unwilling to face the challenge of a living God pulling on the other end of life's rope.

which so many draw back...An impersonal God—well and good. A subjective God of beauty, truth and goodness, inside our own heads—better still. A formless life-force surging through us, a vast power which we can tap—best of all. But God, Himself, alive, pulling at the other end of the cord—that is quite another matter. There comes a moment when the children who have been playing at burglars will hush suddenly: was that a **real** footstep in the hall? There comes a moment when people who have been dabbling in religion...suddenly draw back. Supposing we really found Him? We never meant it to come to **that**! Worst still; supposing He has found us?—**Miracles**, pp. 96, 97.

And so we go through trouble, ulcers, sleepless nights, and finally end up teetering on the edge of the Golden Gate Bridge, ready to abandon life completely.

God's plan is the short route. We let Him find us by coming deliberately into the presence of His love, by taking time to study and contemplate the life, character, and teaching of Jesus Christ. In this short route, we'll be given a sense of need that perhaps a lifetime will not accomplish otherwise.

If you realize that you might be running from God, even if you've been a church member for years, and would like to find Him now, then continue to place yourself in the environment where God can do His work. Associate with others who are interested in seeking the deeper Christian life and study with them. Go to that church service, that worship, that occasion where God might be especially at work, where the Holy Spirit will be able to get through to you. Go to your knees before His Word and meditate on the life of Christ.

Don't run. To the best of your ability, ask God to give you the grace to keep from running. Faith and grace are gifts from God, and He's willing to give them to anyone who asks. You cannot change your heart; you cannot regenerate yourself. You can't even convert yourself, but you can at least let God reach you.

Don't wait for the right speaker to come along. Don't wait for your life to change for the better. Don't wait until you have gone through a long, hard life of suffering and trouble. I'd like to invite you to take your Bible off your shelf, wipe away the dust, and read a chapter **each day** in the Gospels on the life of Christ. When you've finished, start over again, seeking new insights, praying about what you've read. Give God a chance. He's constantly looking for that moment in which you'll give Him an opening.

If you seek to know God with all your heart, you'll find Him, for "never a prayer is offered, however faltering, never a tear is shed, however secret, never a sincere desire after God is cherished, however feeble, but the Spirit of God goes forth to meet it. Even before the prayer is uttered or the yearning of the heart made known, grace from God goes forth to meet the grace that is working upon the human soul"—**Christ's Object Lessons**, p. 206.

I'm thankful for a God who is out looking for me each day, aren't you? I want to let Him catch me, not just at the beginning of my Christian life, but all the way through. Will you join me in seeking that living personal experience with Him?

Dear Father in Heaven, some of us have spent a lot of time thinking we were trying to find You, when we were actually running away. Thank You for following us, for not giving up on us. We pray that we will be drawn closer and closer to You each day, that we may find You and have rest unto our souls. We thank You for Your great provision of mercy and love, in Jesus' name, Amen.

4

Sorry Enough to Quit!

Have you ever been told to tell someone that you were sorry, when you weren't really sorry? Did being told to say that you were sorry make you sorry? No, it probably only made you sorry that you were told to say that you were sorry!

Sometimes we believe repentance, or sorrow for sin and turning away from it, to be a work that takes place only at the beginning of the Christian life. Do we need to turn away from sin only at the beginning, or is it a continuing experience in the life of the Christian?

Trying to understand repentance can be a very elusive pursuit. You ask someone, "How do I turn away from my sins?"

He will answer, "Repent."

"What does that mean?"

"It means to be sorry for your sins."

"Is that all there is to it?"

"Well, it also means turning away from sins."

"Yes, but **how** do I do that?"

"You turn away from your sins by repenting!"

And you could keep up this frustrating dialogue with almost as many people as you could contact. I've tried it. The conclusion is that the way to repent is to turn from your sins, and the way to turn from your sins is to repent. That isn't very helpful to the struggling sinner!

The truth is that the Bible talks about two kinds of repentance. II Corinthians 7:10: "Godly sorrow works repentance to salvation not to be repented of: but the sorrow of the world works death." Godly sorrow makes you sorry enough to quit, but worldly sorrow isn't worth a dime, because it is only being sorry you got caught.

Esau once carefully sought repentance with tears, but he found no place for real sorrow in spite of the tears. Judas felt enough remorse and fear of judgment to kill himself, but he did not have genuine repentance. So the strong exercise of a person's feelings may not indicate that he has repented. In fact, it may be one of the devil's counterfeits.

Then what causes true repentance? What is the kind of genuine repentance or sorrow that changes our lives? I suppose that we have all had some experiences in our lives that have demonstrated the real kind.

It was a warm spring day in Philadelphia, Pennsylvania. I was in the third grade. Very dusty and sweaty, we boys came in from recess and went into the boys' washroom to clean up, forgetting that an upper-grade classroom was still in session. We didn't realize all the noise we were making, until the teacher from that room burst into the boys' washroom and exclaimed, "What's the matter with you, anyway? You sound like a bunch of wild animals!"

Well, I didn't think **she** had any business being in the boys' washroom and I didn't like the way she was addressing us; so I smarted off to her: "That's right, that's what we are."

Thinking that was a little too smart for my britches, she told my teacher, who came to me and said, "I want you to go and tell Miss K. that you are sorry."

But I wasn't sorry. Now, how do you become sorry when you're not sorry? My teacher's telling me to tell Miss K. that I was sorry certainly didn't make me sorry! So I didn't go.

The next day when I arrived at school, my teacher met me. "Did you tell Miss K. you were sorry?"

Now I was in trouble. And the only thing to do in that kind of situation was to add insult to injury, and so I said, "Yes, I did."

But she had the goods on me: "I just checked with Miss K., and she said you didn't."

Now I was in worse trouble, and the only thing I could think of was a pretty weak answer: "Yes, I **did** ... but she must not have heard me!"

My teacher dropped the issue there and said nothing more about it. Time went by and we moved away. The incident was

Too often we define repentance as sorrow for sin, and sorrow for sin as repentance.

forgotten, until the year that I started reading my Bible through. The more I read, the more certain things—including the lie I told to my teacher—began coming back to my conscience. Have you ever had this happen?

So one day I had to sit down and write her a letter about it, asking her to forgive me. For some reason, I was sorry for telling the lie.

What causes a person to be sorry? It wasn't too clear to me at this particular point as I read my Bible through, but I've thought about it often since.

As I continued to read my Bible, I discovered that repentance, or being sorry enough to change, is not something that we can do of ourselves. We cannot manufacture godly sorrow. No matter how hard we try, the power isn't in us! Then where do

55

we get repentance? The source of godly sorrow is suggested in Acts 5;31: "Him (Jesus) has God exalted with His right hand to be a Prince and a Saviour, for to **give** repentance to Israel, and forgiveness of sins."

Forgiveness is a gift! Repentance is a **gift**. Christ **gives** me the ability to become sorry. Repentance is no less the gift of God than are pardon and justification, and it cannot be experienced except as it is given to the soul by Christ.

It is interesting to notice that in the book **Steps to Christ**, there are three major places where it says, "On this point is where many have erred," or "thousands have gone astray." The first one states:

> ... here is a point on which many may err, and hence they fail of receiving the help that Christ desires to give them. They think that they cannot come to Christ unless they first repent.... But must the sinner wait till he has repented before he can come to Jesus? Is repentance to be made an obstacle between the sinner and the Saviour (p. 26)?

Thousands of people have it backwards. They think they have to repent in order to come to Christ, in order for Christ to accept them, but this passage says that we have to come in order to receive repentance!

Then what are we supposed to do?

> The Bible does not teach that the sinner must repent before he can heed to the invitation of Christ, 'Come unto me ... and I will give you rest.' ... We can no more repent without the Spirit of Christ to awaken the conscience than we can be pardoned without Christ (p. 26).

This same chapter tells us:

> If you see your sinfulness, do not wait to make yourself better. How many there are who think they are not good enough to come to Christ. Do you expect to become better through your own efforts?... There is help for us only in God.... We can do nothing of ourselves. We must come to Christ just as we are (p. 31).

All right, then, what do you do in order to repent? You don't waste any time in coming to Christ. That holds true at the beginning of our Christian life and it is also a continuing need for Christian experience.

All our efforts to generate repentance ourselves are destined to fall into failure.

If I have been a Christian for a long time, but still continually fail in some behavioral area of my Christian life, what do I need? I need repentance. How do I get it? Waiting two weeks for God to cool off after I fail before I come back to Him? No! I come to Christ immediately, because He is the only One who can give me the capacity to become sorry enough to change.

Repentance is a continuing transformation; in fact, at every advance step in our Christian experience our repentance will deepen. Repentance is continually turning from self to Christ, and we need to turn to Him every day. This is no one-time experience. I need repentance today, tomorrow, the next day, and God has promised to give it to me.

Does this promise apply only to a few who are elected or chosen? The Lord is not willing that **any** should perish, but that all should come to repentance" (II Peter 3:9). Notice the phrasing of the statement "**come to** repentance." **All** can come. And it is nothing that I can **do**; it is something I come to. I would like to suggest that coming to Christ and coming to repentance are one and the same thing, because when I come to Christ then I receive the repentance that He gives me. Therefore, in living the Christian life, if I continue to come to Christ, I will continue to repent, and the result will be genuine, godly sorrow for sins and a turning away from them.

God calls every person to repentance. The Saviour is continually drawing men to repentance; they need only to submit to be drawn, and their hearts will be melted in penitence. I want that kind of repentance in my own life. Don't you want it, too?

In order to realize the loving acceptance of God, we have to make some effort. What kind of effort does God require of us before He can give us repentance? Many people think that we have to be good, that we have to make an effort to better ourselves, but the truth is that **our effort is to respond by coming to Him as He calls us.**

But how do we come? Some people think it means coming to the front of the church or coming to the preacher. Some think it is coming to a resolution never to do certain things again. The phrase "come to Christ" is intangible, because we can't see Him. There are many ideas as to what constitutes coming to Christ, but the truth is that coming to Christ involves nothing more or less than coming to His Word and to prayer.

If an altar call brings a group of people to the front of the church, but leaves them without knowing what it means to come to Christ themselves, on their knees, individually, the next day and the one after that, then they have not come to Christ for long. Coming to Christ is no deeper than your own personal devotional life with Him. We come to Christ by studying His life, character, and teaching in His Word, and by praying.

One of the first things that He inspires in us **after we come** is a sense of need, helplessness, and great unworthiness, which results in repentance. Repentance is a **gift**. It is not something that I do; rather, it is something that I can't help doing if I come to Christ, because a knowledge of the plan of salvation will lead the sinner to the foot of the cross in repentance for his sins, which have caused the sufferings of God's dear Son. It is when
58

**Repentance is God's gift,
received only in relationship with Him.**

we most fully comprehend the love of God that we best realize the sinfulness of sin.

Repentance is not feeling sorry that I have broken a rule or a law. It is being sorry that I have disappointed the One who gave His life for me. And I have to come to Him and know Him on a daily one-to-one basis in order to realize what I am doing to Him when I continue in my sinning.

So everything in living the Christian life eventually boils down to one thing—the personal relationship with Christ, and this is where repentance ultimately gets pinpointed. Study God's Word prayerfully. That Word convinces of sin. It is when we most fully comprehend the love of God that we best realize the sinfulness of sin. A knowledge of the plan of salvation will lead me to the foot of the cross in repentance, not only at the beginning of my life, but also in my continuing Christian life experience.

My father used to tell me, "Son, there are a lot of people, including Bible characters, who have done many things wrong. But never forget this: the difference between the righteous and the wicked is that the righteous know how to be sorry."

And I've pondered that a lot of times. One of the great evidences of genuine repentance is found in the story of David. We read about it in his great penitential Psalm 51, which gives us clues as to the way he became sorry. Notice that he faced the problem just as it was, without alibis or excuses. "Wash **me** thoroughly from my iniquity and cleanse **me** from my sin" (vs. 2). David realized and confessed his need and helplessness to do anything about being worthy of forgiveness or in cleansing himself. He wasn't just praying about his sins or wrong deeds. He was also praying about his separation from God, his sinful condition, or his evil heart. This was more than simply a desire for pardon of one bad deed; it was also a plea for purity of heart and life.

It took David some rough experiences to realize that he was capable of doing any sin. I remember talking to someone who had experienced a great change for the better in his life, and he said, "One of the great needs I discovered before I could change was to realize what a desperate sinner I was."

"Oh, you were doing desperate things?"

"No, but I had to come to the place where I realized that I was capable of doing any sin."

And evidently the experiences of David proved it. So now he prayed not just for forgiveness of his sins; he prayed for cleansing of himself as well.

Another clue to the godly kind of repentance is also found in Psalm 51: "Against Thee, Thee only, have I sinned." David was saying that this great sin was against God. He pled, "Purge me with hyssop, and I shall be clean: wash me, and I shall be whiter than snow....Create in me a clean heart." He didn't want just **forgiveness**. He was sorry enough to quit, because he realized that his greatest sin was against God, and that's why he wanted a clean heart and a right spirit.

So right here in this psalm is the suggestion that godly sorrow involves a person. Worldly sorrow involves only being sorry that I got caught breaking a set of rules. Godly sorrow always

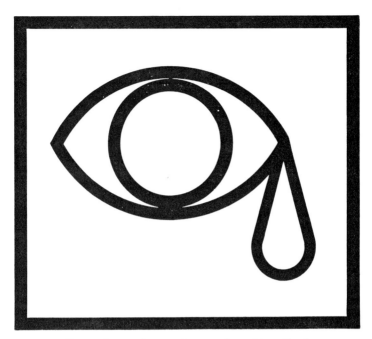

**Repentance issues from a heart touched
with true sorrow for what sin does to a loving God.**

involves a **person** and a broken heart! Being sorry that I broke someone's heart involves looking into the eyes of Jesus—a person, a warm person whose heart is beating in His chest. That's why rules and regulations, that's why the Ten Commandments are not enough. These Ten Commandments are meaningless until they come alive in a person. Then only do you have genuine repentance.

It happened when I was in the seventh grade. My father was holding some meetings in Saginaw, Michigan. There was a little church school of eight grades, with 13 students in the whole school. Our teacher was just 18 years old, and this was her first school. She knew her material all right, but she didn't know how to control and discipline 13 kids. She tried her best, but things got away from her, and midway through the school year, the school board met to see if she should be replaced. Too much anarchy.

Some of the students were talking about her one day out on the playground below the schoolroom window. I came around the corner of the building in time to hear them say they didn't think she was a very good teacher and hoped we'd get a better one. And it's true that even young people aren't happy unless they know what the rules are—where to begin and where to end.

They talked on and on, and when everyone is agreeing on their dislike of the teacher, there is only one thing to do, and that is to join them. So I said, "I don't like her, either. I don't . . . . " And just as I made my speech, there was a movement through the open window I couldn't miss. I looked up, and there was my teacher. She was standing behind the piano where she was sure we couldn't see her. But I could see her, and I will never forget the look of despair on her face. She wasn't looking at us. She was looking at the floor, and I saw the tears streaming down, suddenly I felt sick. I rushed home, and I couldn't sleep very well that night. I had broken someone's heart, someone who had done the best she could for me.

The next day when I got to school, I had to write her a little note and ask her to forgive me. I was really sorry. Why? Because I had broken a rule? No, because I had disappointed a friend. I remembered all the things she had done for us. She had stayed after school to help students in need. She had gone downtown and bought a really worthwhile present for each one of us at Christmastime. She had read us interesting stories every day after lunch. She even taught us a poem by Whittier, which I have never forgotten to this day. Really, it describes repentance:

> Still sits the school house by the road,
> A ragged beggar sunning;
> Around it still the sumachs grow,
> And blackberry vines are running.
>
> Within, the master's desk is seen,
> Deep scarred by raps official;
> The warping floor, the battered seats,
> The jack-knife's carved initial;

The charcoal frescos on the wall;
Its door's worn sill, betraying
The feet that, creeping slow to school,
Went storming out to playing!

Long years ago a winter sun
Shone over it at setting;
Lit up its western window-panes
And low eaves' icy fretting.

It touched the tangled golden curls,
And brown eyes full of grieving,
Of one who still her steps delayed
When all the school were leaving.

For near her stood the little boy
Her childish favor singled;
His cap pulled low upon a face
Where pride and shame were mingled.

Pushing with restless feet the snow,
To right and left, he lingered,—
While restlessly her tiny hands
Her blue-checked apron fingered.

He saw her lift her eyes; he felt
The soft hand's light caressing,
He heard the tremble of her voice,
As if a fault confessing.

'I'm sorry that I spelt the word;
I hate to go above you,
Because,—the brown eyes lower fell,—
'Because, you see, I love you!'

Still memory to a gray-haired man
That sweet child-face is showing.
Dear girl! the grasses on her grave
Have forty years been growing!

He lives to learn, in life's hard school,
How few who pass above him
Lament their triumph and his loss,
Like her,—because they love him.

She was sorry that she spelled the word he couldn't. Why? Because she loved him. And our teacher's message of love had gradually begun to come through. When I remembered all of the things she had done for us, seeing her heart broken because of my ingratitude broke my heart. I wasn't sorry because I had been caught breaking a school rule. It was because I had broken the heart of someone who loved me. I was glad that she was allowed to finish out the year. I was glad to try to be different for her sake. I was glad when I heard the other day that she is still teaching! I haven't seen her since that year, but I'm hoping to see her again.

When someone turns his back on me, when someone disappoints me, when someone talks about me below the schoolroom window, I don't usually feel like welcoming him back. But Jesus does. He accepts thieves, harlots, and moneychangers, inviting them to come to Him for rest and peace. When we really understand the goodness involved in all His blessings, patience, and long-suffering, this breaks our hearts and causes us to be truly sorry and want to change. Who is desirous of becoming truly repentant? What must he do? He must come to Jesus, just as he is, without delay.

Now, the people in the days of Christ had the idea that has continued ever since that day. They thought that

> ... before God's love is extended to the sinner, he must
> first repent. In their view, repentance is a work by
> which men earn the favor of Heaven. And it was this
> thought that led the Pharisees to exclaim in astonish-
> ment and anger, 'This man receiveth sinners.' Accord-
> ing to their ideas He should permit none to approach
> Him but those who had repented (**Christ's Object
> Lessons**, p. 189).

Well, if that's true, then there is no hope for any of us. If He never received sinners, there would never have been a chance for you or me. But He accepts us—at the beginning of our Christian life and all the way through. And His goodness in accepting us breaks our hearts, because it isn't human to love and accept people who hate you. Jesus died for his enemies and promised
64

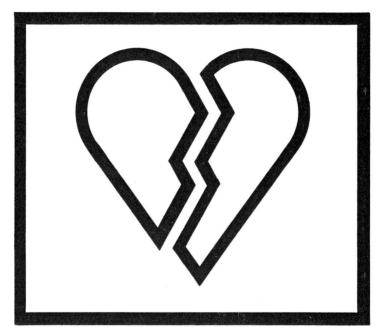

**Repentance views sin not as breaking a rule,
but as breaking a heart—God's.**

that "him that cometh to me I will in no wise cast out"—John 6:37.

God's loving attitude of acceptance creates in us the desire to change our lives. He always accepts anyone, any time, any place, regardless of his past, who comes to Him. Remember, the unpardonable sin is not God's turning us down; it is our turning God down. And so the word comes to every despondent soul to take courage,

> ... even though you have done wickedly. Do not think that **perhaps** God will pardon your transgressions and permit you to come into His presence. God has made the first advance. While you were in rebellion against Him, He went forth to seek you .... The soul, bruised and wounded and ready to perish, He encircles in His arms

of love—**Christ's Object Lessons**, pp. 188-189.

Not only does God accept those whose lives have been most offensive to Him, but "when they repent, He imparts to them His divine Spirit, places them in the highest positions of trust, and sends them forth into the camp of the disloyal to proclaim His boundless mercy"—**The Desire of Ages**, p. 826. Do you like that? The goodness of God!

I learned it from my father. Evidently, from their "Old Country" traditions, the Norwegians didn't believe in sparing the rod. One day I came in grinning after "getting it" with the newspaper. I said to my mother, "That didn't even hurt." That was my big mistake, for she told my dad, and that's when the hose came off the tire pump. I got many a licking, but I didn't hold it against my father.

Later, I heard a family counselor describe why a person can take discipline: "There is no limit to the discipline that anyone, young or old, can take as long as he still knows that he is loved and accepted. The minute he feels rejected, you've gone too far. That's the only limitation." We always knew that we were loved and accepted. We knew father's heart was breaking when he had to discipline us, because we needed it.

But the worst licking I ever got was the time he never even touched me. It was one summertime. Camp Pottawatomie at Gull Lake was on the middle of an island. It was a summer camp in Michigan. Father and Mother were trying to help us have a good time. We had everything. My brother and I had the canoes, the waterfront, the speedboats, swimming, and **each other**. That's where the problem was. They call it "sibling rivalry" now. I don't know what they called it then. We called it fighting.

It would start out in innocent fun, but always ended in a brawl. Fight, fight, fight. Ruining the vacation for Father and Mother. Father tried lickings, he tried depriving us of our waterfront privileges, he tried making us go without dessert, he tried making us go without supper. Nothing worked. We were still at each other's throats. Finally he called us into the cabin. We sat down on the edge of the bed, wondering what would be next. But he had obviously run out of solutions. Nothing more to do. He tried to think of something. Nothing else. He tried to talk. Nothing to say. And then, for one of the few times in my life, I saw tears start down the face of my big, strong father. Now, I

**By beholding and experiencing Christ,
true repentance grows in the Christian life.**

could take the razor strap and the hose off the tire pump, but I couldn't take my father's tears. I was really sorry that time. Why? Because I realized that I had broken the heart of my best friend, the one who had done so much for me. I really wanted to change. And we did; my brother and I became close friends.

What made the difference? I've thought about these personal experiences and what repentance is all about. How do you become sorry? You realize that you've broken the heart of someone who loves you and this breaks your heart. That's where the real lifeblood of repentance is. Romans 2:4 tells us that the goodness of God leads us to repentance. And it goes something like this:

1. You realize that you are a sinner, capable of disappointing someone else.

2. You realize that God loves you and that He is your Friend because you learn to know Him personally.

3. When you do something that disappoints Him, it disappoints you, too.

4. When you realize that even though He is disappointed, that His power, mercy, and patience are still there, and that He still accepts you back, this breaks your heart. It's not human, it can only be **divine**!

Remember, friend, there's no such thing as changing your life apart from a relationship of closeness with Christ, because this is the only way to become sorry enough to quit. I couldn't take the broken heart of my friend. Neither could Peter, one of Christ's disciples.

One night as he stood by the open fire, a maid accused him of being a disciple of Jesus. And then he began to curse and swear, "I don't know Him." Right in the midst of his denials, his eyes focused upon the eyes of Jesus. The look in Jesus' eyes was not one of anger or resentment. It was a look that only Heaven could have produced. It was more than a look of sorrow and disappointment, for it was also one of pity and acceptance for His poor disciple. And as Peter stood there transfixed with his eyes on Jesus, he saw the pale, suffering face, he saw the quivering lips stained with bloody sweat and convulsed with anguish. He watched as people pushed Him around, raised evil hands to strike Him, and even spat in His face.

But that wasn't all he saw. A flood of memories came over him, and he recalled the day when Jesus' friendly voice invited him to leave his nets and follow Him; the night when he, because of his own braggadocio, wanted to walk on the water and Jesus saved him from the crashing billows before he sank; the time in the Temple when he got into an argument about the tax coins and Jesus was there to save him again. He also remembered, just a few hours before, his boasting to Jesus that "You can count on me, even if everyone else runs away! I won't leave You!" And Jesus had replied, "Peter, Satan would like to have you, that he could sift you as wheat, but I have prayed for you. I have prayed that your faith fail not."

Suddenly, through tear-dimmed eyes, Peter realized that he had struck the hardest blow on Jesus that night. He fled from the fireside and out through the gate, down through the dark streets of Jerusalem to the golden gate in the city wall, down the hill, across the brook Kedron and up into the olive trees, the site of the garden of Gethsemane. There he groped in the darkness until he found the very spot where Jesus had been in anguish just a few hours before. And he fell on his face and wished that he could die. He was really sorry. Why? Because he had broken the heart of his best Friend.

Peter lived. He wanted to die, but he lived. And when he later stood before thousands of people and invited them to come to Christ for repentance, he knew what he was talking about. When you and I realize this kind of sorrow for sin, then we will have received the gift that Jesus offers. Then we are filled with the longing to know His presence and power in such a way that we no longer disappoint Him. That's how lives are changed. This is how victory is experienced.

Listen, friend, there's no chance that I can change my life. Only God can do it, and there's no chance that He can do it for me until I realize Him as my personal Friend and realize what my life means to Him. Can you accept that?

I would like to have a deeper experience of repentance each day. I invite you to seek to know God better, too.

> Dear Father in Heaven, thank You for Your great love. It's not human. We can't understand it, for we can't operate that way apart from You, without Your presence. Thank You for seeking us when we've gone astray, and thank You for Your invitation to come in repentance, to repentance, for repentance. We know that You are the only One who can make us sorry enough to quit. Help us experience the relationship with You that causes repentance to happen. Thank You for Your forgiveness and mercy, and help us to keep on coming like Peter.

5

A Spiritual Prescription

Is it easier to become or to remain a Christian? In asking people, both young and old, I've found that they usually think it's more difficult to remain a Christian. Perhaps they'd experienced conversion after an evangelistic rally or religious retreat; maybe they were touched by a hymn or a sermon. But after a while, the feeling died down, and they were back where they'd been before. Or maybe they discovered the futility of working on their righteousness or their faith. And they've become discouraged. Why is this so? Could it be that they don't understand **how** to live the Christian life? What is the basis of the Christian life?

Whether you are a teenager or whether you have white hair and arthritis, these same questions probably face you today. How can Christianity become meaningful in your life? How can you get to know Jesus personally? I'd like to tell you how the Christian life became tangible to me.

After being in the ministry for three years, I came into great trouble. Up to then, I had successfully borrowed sermons from other preachers, including father and uncle; I'd managed to preach about last-day events and church doctrine. But then one day I realized that there was nothing of my own thinking and experience with Christ in these talks. I'd gone through the motions and routines all my life without really knowing what this whole business of Christianity was about. Now, as a minister, I was supposed to be an authority on it.

One day I tried to preach about Jesus, and that's when I discovered that I was caught in the trap of trying to talk about Someone I didn't know personally. And when I realized that the essence of the gospel was supposed to be Jesus but that my focus wasn't on Him, things began to look pretty bleak. Believe me, there's nothing more frustrating than being a minister of the gospel when you don't know Jesus! As I developed ulcers, I became painfully aware that unless I knew Jesus Christ through a personal experience, I'd better look for another job.

I decided to quit and dig ditches, but I knew that if I left the ministry, I'd also probably walk away from religion entirely. After having grown up on the "sawdust trail," I couldn't help believing that someday the Holy City of God would come down from Heaven—and that everyone who ever lived or died would meet for the first and last time. Some would be on the inside of the city, but most would be on the outside. I thought that if I ended up with the majority on the outside, it would be nice to know that I'd done my best to find out what religion was all about. Then I'd be able to shake my fist at God and say, "I did everything I knew. It's Your fault, not mine, that I'm out here. You'd better open up the gates and let me in, anyhow."

So I determined to do the best I could to find out the answers to this business of Christianity. At campmeeting, it was the job of the ministers to pitch the tents. That's how they got their yearly exercise, and they'd soon get exhausted. After the first few tents were up, they'd hide behind them to nurse their injuries and spend time in theological discussions. I remember some of the topics were rather insignificant: what happens to a flower in Heaven if you pick it? Do angels really have wings? Etc. I became haunted by those discussions, because apparently the assumption was that everyone knew all about Christianity; so we could spend our time talking about trivia and things having nothing to do with our salvation. Meanwhile, people were wanting to know that their sins were forgiven and that they could have the certainty of acceptance with God.

So I got some of these ministers aside one by one and asked questions concerning faith and religion and how it could become real. As a fellow minister, I was too embarrassed to admit that I had personal questions about this; so I approached them from the third person: "Suppose I have someone in my congregation who doesn't understand how to be saved. What
72

"Theological discussions," like the one concerning what happens to a flower picked in Heaven, may be stimulating, but they produce little spiritual growth.

do I tell him?"

And the answers started coming:

"Tell him that he needs to get a new life from above."

"Well, how does he do that?"

"Tell him to reach out his hand and take God's."

"How do I, er, I mean, how does **he** do that?"

"He has to fall on the Rock and be broken."

"What does that mean?"

"It means that he has to behold the Lamb."

"How does he behold the Lamb if he can't see Him?"

"Well, he has to look through the eye of faith."

"And how can he do that?"

"By surrendering his will."

I'm sorry to say that I came home from campmeeting more discouraged than ever. I'd even used some of those intangible phrases in my own counseling and sermons, but they were meaningless to me in my search for concrete answers. And I became painfully aware that much of our religious terminology and jargon probably meant nothing to most other people. These terms were unreal and out of reach for the one who had never experienced them.

I was determined to quit the ministry, but someone said, "You haven't finished searching yet, because you haven't studied for it in books."

And I have to admit that I only read my Bible and prayed when I had to. But I decided to study it again to find the answers, looking for concrete ways of making the intangible phrases more meaningful.

I bought every book there was on the subject of faith, Jesus, victory, and overcoming sins. There wasn't much written at that time, but I came across a book, **Steps to Christ**, that seemed small enough so I could get through all of it without too much difficulty. I had read it for a class before, and it had been boring. But this time I determined to read it all the way through and underline everything it told me to do. I started reading this book, and unfortunately, underlined nearly **everything**. I also discovered where all the intangible phrases had come from: they were all there. By the time I finished the book, I was angry enough to throw it in the fireplace, for these underlined phrases were still unreal and intangible.

But when I paused to think things over, I found something strange had happened inside. I couldn't explain it, but while I felt further away from being able to describe what I was after, I was more determined to keep on searching. I decided to give it one more try, but this time, I would underline **twice** only the concrete things that I could possibly do. Much to my surprise, I underlined only **three** things: Bible study, prayer, and share. And that wasn't pleasant news, because I'd rather have read the telephone directory than the Bible, but I thought I'd better give it a chance.

So I sat down with this little magical recipe for success: read the Bible so much each day and pray a little bit to make God happy. Let this mixture bake in the oven for half an hour, and out comes victory cake. But victory cake didn't come out!

I wondered what was wrong. Then one day I came across the story of Nicodemus. He came to Jesus one night for the purpose of entering into a discussion. He said, "Master, you're a great teacher, and I'd like to discuss some great theological concepts with you."

Have you ever been involved in that trap? He wanted to discuss and dissect and analyze, but Jesus told him that **saving** knowledge came only by knowing God.

So I started over on this formula of studying the Bible and praying, but this time I began to search the Scriptures for the specific purpose of getting acquainted with God, learning to know Jesus, by studying His life and teachings in the Gospels, and it made a difference. I discovered that righteousness was nothing that I could work up. It was a **gift** that came spontaneously as the result of knowing God, of knowing and becoming acquainted with Jesus Christ.

Since then I've looked for other methods of continuing my Christian experience, other ways in which one learns to know Jesus, but I've never found anything else. All other good works are the **result** of this daily time alone with Jesus. I cannot even generate faith in myself; it is a **gift** from God. Therefore the whole basis of the Christian life is to know Jesus and have a one-to-one relationship with Him.

Jesus described the necessity of a daily acquaintance with Him in John 6: "I am the bread of life—the living bread which came down from heaven. He who comes to Me will never hunger and he who believes in Me shall never thirst. If anyone eats my flesh and drinks my blood, he shall live forever, but if he doesn't, he will have no life in him."

Well, that sounds a little confusing, doesn't it? One wonders what the cannibals in the South Seas islands would think if their only contact with Christianity was this description. But Jesus said that He was talking about the spiritual life of the individual: "My words are spirit and life."

And if you'll continue pondering His statements in this chapter, you'll discover that He was talking about the personal, intimate relationship with Him. He was describing the devotional life—in which we dwell in Him and He in us. We are to come into such a close relationship with Him that our will is merged in His. He was telling us that we cannot be living Christians unless we seek Him each day.

One day I came across an interesting comment: "None are living Christians unless they have a daily experience in the things of God." Now, this statement is a little nebulous, because some people would say, "Well, what do you mean by 'the things of God'?"

The legalist would say, "That means we keep the commandments. We have to earn our way into Heaven."

The pseudo-intellectual would say, "Well, that means we have to analyze and dissect all the fine points of theology in order to understand."

The positive thinker might say, "This means making yourself believe all the promises in the Bible, that they will happen if you believe hard enough."

The person of genuine faith would say, "It means to eat Jesus' flesh and drink His blood spiritually, and that refers to a personal experience with Him, based upon a daily contact with Him."

What does that really mean? I once read an interesting comment on John 6 that I'd like to share with you:

The reception of the Word, the Bread from Heaven, is declared to be the reception of Christ Himself. As the Word of God is received into the soul, we partake of the flesh and blood of the Son of God ....

As the blood is formed in the body by the food eaten, so Christ is formed within by the eating of the Word of God, which is His flesh and blood. He who feeds upon that Word has Christ formed within, the hope of glory. The written Word introduces the searcher to the flesh and blood of the Son of God; and through obedience to that Word, he becomes a partaker of the divine nature. As the necessity for temporal food cannot be supplied by once partaking of it, so the Word of God must be daily eaten to supply the spiritual necessities.

As the life of the body is found in the blood, so spiritual life is maintained through faith in the blood of Christ ....

By reason of the waste and loss, the body must be renewed with blood, by being supplied with daily food. So there is need of constantly feeding on the Word, the knowledge of which is eternal life. That Word must be our meat and drink. It is in this alone that the

**A spiritual "prescription" for successful Christian living:
take time alone at the beginning of each day to
fellowship with Jesus Christ.**

soul will find its nourishment and vitality.

Therefore I maintain my Christian experience by spending time alone each day in getting acquainted with God. I live by faith in Christ and abide in Him through His Word and through prayer.

"Well," asks someone, "how do I get acquainted with God if I can't see Him?"

We become acquainted with anyone, including Jesus, by three simple methods. They're the basis of this spiritual prescription I'm suggesting: I become acquainted with you 1) by talking to you and 2) by listening to you talk to me. We become better acquainted 3) by going places together, by working or doing things together.

God has given us these same avenues by which we come into an intimate relationship with Him. I'm only going to get acquainted with Him by learning who He is, by talking to Him (prayer), and by listening to what He has to say (studying His Word). And then we'll do things together (the Christian witness).

I remember holding evangelistic meetings in a little town with my brother. Someone turned in a name of a man who was an interested prospect. He lived out in the country, and I went to see him. When I told him that I was a preacher who had come to town to hold meetings, he said, "Oh, you're one of those blankety-blank preachers!" (And he didn't say "blankety-blank" either!)

And then he invited me in and spent half an hour trying to insult me, shock me, and tear me down. He said, "I've talked to the blankety-blank pillow just as much as you ever did, and I never got any answers."

On and on he went. Finally, at the close of the visit, I asked him to give us a chance—to just come.

He replied, "Yes, I'll come and give you a bad time."

And he kept his word; he kept coming. He couldn't create a new heart within his own chest, but he could do one thing: he could keep coming.

I've had young people tell me that they weren't born again, and they knew they were powerless to change their lives. But I told them they **were** able to do one thing: they could place themselves in an environment where it could happen.

If I am to try to put myself to sleep at night, I can do at least this much: I can put my back against the mattress and turn out the light and turn off the radio. I can place myself in an environment where it will happen, and sooner or later it happens. But it usually won't happen unless I place myself in that kind of environment.

So this man kept on coming to our meetings, in which we did only three things: studied the Bible, prayed, and witnessed to the love of Christ. And one night he came out of those meetings and said, "Say, you fellows have a pretty good sales pitch."

We thought, "Well, that's an interesting way to put it."

A few nights later when he came out of those meetings, his eyes were sort of glistening, and he said, "I guess I do need what Jesus has to offer."

In God's Word, we meet Jesus; by spending time with Him, we come to know Him better—and this is the foundation of spiritual life.

Soon afterwards, he surrendered his life to Christ, and I'll never forget the day when we walked into the baptismal pool together. He was a changed man.

What had happened? He had placed himself in an environment where the flesh and blood of the Son of God became part of his life. I saw him again, years later, and he'd been growing as a Christian, because he had learned how to spend this time alone with Christ. He had learned that "sinful man can find hope and righteousness only in God, and no human being is righteous any longer than he has faith in God and maintains a vital connection with Him."

Although the sum and substance of the Christian life is being acquainted with Jesus each day, we often don't believe that it's that easy. The devil tries to get us to work on our righteousness and our faith, and usually after we've spent our time battling the enemy, we don't have any time left over for getting acquainted with Jesus. We are told that the whole armor of God is necessary in order to be victorious (Ephesians 6:11-17), but we don't realize that the armor is really Christ Jesus put on us (Romans 13:14).

Therefore we continue our Christian experience and life by knowing what it means to get on our knees before God's open Word, day by day. There is no other way to know God, except through the personal, private devotional life.

Now, I make no apologies for writing about this specifically. The absence of a meaningful devotional life in the lives of many professed Christians is quite marked. I've known of ministers who have become discouraged, because their church members have come face to face with real problems, and when they run to the preacher for help, they'll admit that they haven't spent any time in studying the Gospels and spending time alone with Christ.

My question to you today, whoever you are, is this: "Do you know what it means to have a meaningful personal devotional time with God each day?"

Now, it's possible for a legalist to think that he is spending time in getting acquainted with Jesus, when he's really looking for information to debate, discuss, or argue. It's possible that I can spend a thoughtful hour in contemplation of passages that will make clear the faults and the deficiencies of others' beliefs and practices. But that's not a meaningful devotional life, for my focus isn't on God.

I remember a little old lady who had a practice of studying for hours with the purpose of finding things she could use to club other people over the head with. If you were to ask her if she had a devotional life with Christ, why, of course she'd say she did.

But I remember the day another little old lady came to church with her two granddaughters. At the beginning of that week, the girls came to visit, and they presented Grandma with a present they had made themselves: two necklaces of beads from the local dimestore. Now, Grandma didn't believe in wearing beads, especially to church; so she thanked the two girls and put the beads in her top drawer.

Spiritual growth is like falling asleep: you can't "make it happen," but you can place yourself in an environment where it CAN happen.

When the end of the week came, she asked them if they'd go to church with her, and the granddaughters replied, "Yes, Grandma. Will you wear our necklaces?"

She didn't know what to do—and whether she did the right thing is not for me to decide—but she put the beads on, then pulled the collar of her coat over her neck and came to church. **That**, of course, immediately attracted the attention of the pious little lady.

The pious one met the grandma on the steps after church, reached under her coat collar, and yanked the strings off her neck. The beads fell on the sidewalk, and two little granddaughters bent down to pick them up. For some reason, they never again wanted to go to church there.

I went to see the pious lady and said, "Do you know what it means to spend time alone getting acquainted with God?

"Oh, yes." And she pulled out all the books she'd been reading. She had plenty, with markers in all of them. In fact, she'd been sending me quotations of what was wrong with the church, but I found that the contemplation of the life and the character of Jesus was conspicuously absent.

What is this devotional life? It's a special time in which I seek to become acquainted with God. I've never found a better method of approach than to spend a thoughtful hour each day in contemplation of the life and teachings of Christ as recorded in the Gospels.

"Oh," objects someone, "but what about the rest of the Bible? What about the doctrines of our church?"

Listen, friend, there are two types of information in the Bible: one is for instruction; one is for inspiration. God will guide us to the instructional parts of the Bible if we seek Him, but they are no substitutes for the passages that will help you know Jesus Christ as your personal Friend.

This time alone with Him is something more than a text for the day with my hand on the doorknob. It is reading His Word for communication, then pondering what I've read. I read of His encounter with people who were no different from you and me today. Then I pray about what I've read, putting myself in the picture. I'm the leper who was healed; I'm the blind man whose sight was restored. And as I personalize what I've read, I will learn to know Him.

Family worship and church are wonderful. They can be meaningful. But they are blessings only if each of us has a personal connection with God. And God prefers us to ask for power in the morning to go through the day, rather than to ask forgiveness for neglecting Him at the end of each day.

Now, some people object to this prescription, because it is inconvenient. Some say, "Oh, I just simply communicate with God all day long. I can pray at work. I keep in touch with Him all through the day."

"Yes, but do you have a certain time of your day set aside for special personal communication with Him?"

"No, I don't need that."

Now, I think it's wonderful to keep in touch with God all through the day. In fact that's the purpose of the time set aside
82

A thoughtful hour spent each day contemplating the life of Christ can revolutionize your spiritual experience.

with God. We don't box Him into a little hour-long corner, but make the contact that will keep us in touch all day long. But I've discovered that usually when a person says, "I just keep in touch with Him all through the day, but have no special time alone with God," he's really saying something about the shallowness of his experience, for Jesus said that you cannot have spiritual life unless you take special time for spiritual food.

It would be ridiculous if I told my doctor, "I don't need to eat. I don't need three meals a day. Why, I've found that I can just naturally be nourished all through the day.

It doesn't make sense in the physical realm, for the nourishment and replacement that goes on in the human body takes place as a **result** of having special times for meals. And it is just as foolish in the Christian life to say, "Well, I don't have to spend

time with Him. I just naturally keep in touch through the day."
In fact, I'd like to take the position that where the deeper Christian life is concerned, you don't really keep that close to God all through the day unless you have a specific time to spend alone with Him.

"Well," says someone else, "I don't have enough time to spend in that."

Listen, my friend, if you don't have time to pray and seek God, then you have no time to live, for God can't teach you anything unless you spend time with Him. I'll **guarantee** you that if you will spend time alone with God each day, He'll see that you are much more efficient in everything else you do.

I'll never forget the experience through which I discovered this for myself. I had just begun to understand the importance of spending time alone with God each day. Now I was one of those in charge of the youth tent at a campmeeting. We'd have programs through the day, then an evening meeting as well. After that was over, we'd have a staff meeting in which we'd discuss plans and problems for the next day's events. And by the time we finished, it was 11:00 at night. Because of all the work that had to be done **before** the morning sessions, I discovered that I would have to get up at 4:30 a.m. in order to have some meaningful time alone with God.

And so I asked God that if He wanted me to spend time with Him, to wake me up at 4:30. I threw out my alarm clock and went to bed. All of a sudden I woke with a start. I looked at my watch, and the second hand was just sweeping past 4:30!

Now, psychiatrists might say that I managed to manipulate my mind to wake myself up, but I doubt it. If you'll study the life of Christ, you'll find that He was awakened each morning by God in order to prepare Him for the new day (Isaiah 50:4).

I've discovered that if I have to miss sleep in order to spend time alone with God, He'll give me two hours of strength for the one hour lost from my rest. Isaiah 40:28-31 says that He gives strength to the faint.

This spiritual prescription of taking **time alone** at the **beginning** of **every day** to fellowship with Jesus Christ may sound mystical and unreal. Many of us are so locked in on measuring our Christianity by our behavior—by the externals of dos and don'ts—that we find it difficult to switch to **relationship**. Often we've started out in total faith and dependence upon Christ,
84

Putting on "the armor of Christ" actually means nothing more or less than putting on Christ Himself!

but after a while, we've thought we were expected to live a good life apart from Him.

And the externals are more tangibly understood. There's no question about it. When a behaviorist tries to switch to relationship, he still looks for something to happen immediately as the result of this time alone with Christ. When instant victory doesn't happen, he skips a week, then tries again. On-again, off-again religion. Then he says, "Well, your spiritual prescription doesn't work!"

Of course not! You can have just enough religion to make you miserable but not enough to be saved. But Luke 9:23 tells us that this personal experience with Christ has to be a **daily** matter in order to be meaningful and living.

God wants us to get acquainted with Him, and then do what

85

is right as the **result** of having His power within us. And all of the intangible phrases that are used to describe the Christian experience are made tangible and real through our personal daily devotional life with Christ.

Now, it is possible to simply engage in this time alone each day as one more duty required to enter Heaven. Just because a person eats and breathes does not mean he is going to be healthy. But he isn't going to be healthy if he doesn't eat and breathe. And just because a person reads his Bible and prays each day doesn't mean he will have a healthy Christian experience. But there is no other way that he can learn to know God personally in his own life, apart from this daily experience.

I'd like to suggest to you that, regardless of how you **feel**, you can start tomorrow morning with this experience of getting acquainted with Christ. If you take your Bible and read of the life and character of Christ, realizing your need of His presence in your life, and if you will continue your search regardless of what happens, gradually there will be a change, and you'll begin to look forward to this quiet time alone with God. I've seen it happen in my own life and in the lives of others.

If you will seek fellowship with Christ each day, enabling Him to dwell in you and work in you, you'll discover the reality that:

> Nothing is apparently more helpless, yet really more invincible, than the soul that feels its nothingness and relies wholly on the merits of the Saviour. By prayer, by the study of His Word, by faith in His abiding presence, the weakest of human beings may live in contact with the living Christ, and He will hold them by a hand that will never let go—**The Ministry of Healing**, p. 182.

> Dear Father in Heaven, forgive us for relying upon ourselves for goodness and righteousness, and for neglecting the basics in the Christian life. Guide us to a meaningful time alone with You each day. If it looks hard and mechanical, take us on through, and help us to learn to seek You, not just for solutions to all our sins and problems, but for the joy of actual communication and fellowship with You. Help us to learn our need for You each day of our lives, in Jesus' name, we pray, Amen.

6

The Patience of God

I once saw an inscription on an early American grave: "Here lies Lem S. Frame, who killed 89 Indians in his life. He was hoping to have killed 100 by the end of the year when he fell asleep in Jesus in his house at Hawk's Ferry." And as I read that, I sensed something was wrong. Someone misunderstood the character of God.

When I was a college student, a group of us went to the Hollywood Bowl to hear a famous preacher whose subject included the smell of brimstone and the shrieks of hell. He had an altar call, and people came down to the front, pleading for mercy from an angry God. That night as we came home, our car was struck by lightning. I remember how quiet we were the rest of the way home, wondering if God wasn't mad at us for going to that meeting. Is this the way God operates?

Some people have said to me, "I sort of like Jesus, but I don't like God!"

"Why not?"

"Because Jesus is merciful, but God is stern and full of wrath!"

Is this a true picture of God? The proper blend of God's love and justice has been debated for a long time. The cheap brand of Christianity pictures Him as being love, sweetness, and light—a God who never harms anyone and who will eventually let everyone into Heaven. The other extreme views God as being harsh, severe, and looking for every chance He can get to destroy His creatures. And only a few will be able to escape the doom of a fiery hell.

This misunderstanding of God's character has caused many people to stay away from religion. I've met people who were unbelievers because they had been given the wrong picture of God. If they had accepted the version that many have been taught to believe about God, I think God Himself would have been unhappy.

When asked why he denied the existence of God, one well-known man replied, "I'm an agnostic because I am not afraid to think. I'm not afraid of any god in the universe who would send me or any other human being to hell. If there were such a being, he would not be God. He would be a devil!"

And that's pretty good thinking, except this man didn't bother to study the Bible to find out the truth about God.

The apostle Paul tells us that God's character has been misunderstood and misinterpreted since the beginning of the world. People knew something about Him once, but they didn't glorify Him as God. As a result they

> ... became vain in their imaginations, and their foolish heart was darkened. Professing themselves to be wise, they became fools, And changed the glory of the uncorruptible God into an image made like to corruptible man, and to birds, and to fourfooted beasts, and creeping things—Romans 1:20-23.

It is possible for us to change God into something else than He really is, even if we don't bow down to idols of wood and stone. If we don't have the proper understanding of His character, then we're worshiping a false God! We understand that the last rays of merciful light, the last message of mercy to be given to the world, is a revelation of His character of love. Unless we know what God is really like, we won't be able to reveal Him to the rest of the world!

Where can we find out about His true character of love and mercy? In John 14, Jesus told His disciples, "If you know Me, then you know My Father also."

Philip said, "Show us the Father."

Jesus replied, "Have I been with you all this time, and yet you have not known Me? If you've seen Me, you've seen the Father. I am in the Father and He is in Me. The words and the works that I do are My Father's, for He dwells in Me."

What was Jesus' mission? Why did He come? Jesus came to a world that was in complete misapprehension of God, in order

One of the most important concepts for Christians to grasp is the true relationship between God's love and God's justice.

to demonstrate what the Father is really like—what He has always been like and always will be like.

One day Jesus and His disciples passed by a blind man (John 9). The disciples asked, "Master, who sinned? This man or his parents, that he was born blind?"

Their question was based on the common concept of God and evil. The people of Christ's day believed that disease and death were God's arbitrary punishment for a wrongdoing, either by the sufferer himself or his parents. Because of this, the suffering person had the additional burden of being considered a great sinner.

Jesus corrected their error by explaining that sickness and pain are caused by Satan. But one of the devil's clever traps is to project his own attributes onto God instead, and as a result,

89

millions of people through the centuries have blamed God for suffering, sickness, and death.

One day Jesus passed through some Samaritan villages on His way to Jerusalem. When His disciples requested permission to stay overnight, one village refused, and the disciples asked Jesus to call down fire from Heaven to destroy the Samaritans. Jesus replied, "You don't know your spirit. You're siding with the devil, not Me, for the Son of man didn't come to destroy men's lives, but to save them"—Luke 9:56.

John 3:16, 17 tells us that God loved the world enough to send His own Son to redeem us. He "sent not His son into the world to condemn the world, but that the world through Him might be saved." That's the gospel! That's redemption!

Another time, some people came to Jesus to tell of a great massacre. There had been popular uprisings against Pontius Pilate, the governor of Judea, and in order to restore order to the province, he allowed his soldiers to invade the temple to kill Galilean pilgrims who were in the very act of offering sacrifices to God.

When the Jews told Jesus about this calamity, they didn't feel pity or sympathy; rather, they felt deep down inside a sense of satisfaction: "Since this tragedy didn't happen to us, then we must be better and more favored by God than those Galileans."

Jesus knew their inner thoughts and rebuked them by saying, "I suppose you think this tragedy happened because they were greater sinners than you. Not so! All of you have great problems, too, and unless you repent, all of you will perish"—Luke 13:1-5.

Jesus is not here ignoring the justice of God. In fact, it is an important thing to consider the justice and judgment of God, as well as His mercy. Let us look also at the other side of God's character.

In modern days, we have seen great disasters that might indicate God's judgments. I remember reading about the tremendous upheaval of Mt. Pelee on the island of Martinique in the West Indies in 1902. The capital city, St. Pierre, was completely destroyed. Only two persons survived, and one was a prisoner in a very deep cell.

It's very interesting to notice what happened just before the volcanic eruption destroyed the city. On the last day, a pig was
90

crucified in mockery of the crucifixion of Christ. Then afterward, another pig was led through the streets in procession to signify the resurrection.

On the morning of the day that St. Pierre was buried in ashes, the newspapers announced a culminating blow at the Christian religion. They said that the sacrament of the Lord's Supper would be administered to a horse. The destruction of the defiant sinners of St. Pierre, along with others who had no part in the blasphemy, may have indeed been a coincidence, but the Bible tells us that in due time, God shall bring every work into judgment.

According to geologists, San Francisco might slough off into the ocean at any time. This dire prediction has turned out to be somewhat of a comedy and jest among the people of the Bay Area. But the truth is that one of these days we know that mercy will no longer plead and justice must be dealt. The Bible describes times in the past when God "spared not" because His justice could no longer permit conditions to continue as they were. The first time that God "spared not" is recorded in Genesis 18. Abraham, "the friend of God," was bargaining with Him about the fate of Sodom. And apparently he must have had a relationship of deep friendship and closeness with God in order to bargain in this way.

He questioned, "Are you going to destroy the righteous along with the wicked? Suppose there are 50 righteous people within the city. Will you spare it for the righteous that are within?"

And then he appealed to God's sense of fairness by adding, "That be far from Thee to do after this manner, to slay the righteous with the wicked: and that the righteous should be as the wicked, that be far from Thee: shall not the Judge of all the earth do right?"

God was patient with this man who was trying to tell his Creator the proper thing to do, for He answered, "If I find in Sodom fifty righteous within the city, then I will spare all the place for their sakes."

Then Abraham became nervous. Perhaps he had put the stakes too high. What if there weren't 50? So he continued to bargain for a lower number—45, 30, and 20.

Finally he said, "Oh, let not the Lord be angry, and I will speak yet but this once: peradventure ten shall be found there. Will you spare it still?"

As the destruction of Sodom and Gomorrah shows, a
point can be reached where God's justice requires that sin
be dealt with in a direct and final way.

And the Lord replied, "I will not destroy it for ten's sake." God
went His way, and Abraham evidently felt safe, for he returned
to his home, but you know the rest of the story. There weren't
even 10 righteous people in Sodom, and it, along with the city
of Gomorrah, was destroyed. God saw a point in the iniquity
and the rebellion where it could no longer be allowed to continue, because He is a God of justice.

The second time that God "spared not" is found in Romans
11:21. Paul was writing to the Christians at Rome, imploring them
to change their ways. One of his arguments drew a parallel to
the olive tree. He reminded them that even though they were
wild branches that had been grafted onto the olive tree, God
had broken off the natural branches (the Jewish nation),
because there came a point in His mercy and justice where He

When man's sinfulness, in Noah's day, reached a point where God could no longer allow it to continue, He destroyed all but Noah's family in the Great Flood.

could no longer spare the entire nation. After thousands of years of patience and longsuffering, God rejected Israel as His peculiar people. He didn't exclude individuals from salvation, but they were no longer, as a group, His representatives to the rest of the world.

Paul tells us that the final blow came after the Jews rejected God's Son. They were too busy being religious to find any time for their Saviour, the only righteous One (Romans 9:31, 32).

The third instance when God "spared not" because of His justice is described in II Peter 2:5. God "spared not" the old world, but saved only "Noah the eighth person, a preacher of righteousness, bringing in the flood upon the world of the ungodly." Only eight people were spared.

Not even angels could be allowed to sin without judgment. When rebellion broke out in Heaven, many mighty angels were expelled from God's presence.

Why? Genesis 6:5 describes the condition of man at that time as being "evil continually." The world had reached an all-time low, and there came a point in God's justice where He could no longer permit things to continue. If He had ignored all of the evils and wrong, His universe would have disintegrated, for if penalties for wrong are not enforced, the laws can't stand, and if they don't stand, then the government is invalid, and anarchy results. We serve a God who is too intelligent to let that happen!

The fourth time that God "spared not" penetrates the very universe. II Peter 2:4: "For God spared not the angels that sinned, but cast them down to hell, and delivered them into chains of darkness, to be reserved unto judgment." When sin went on in the very presence of God, rebellion broke out in His courts, led by a mighty angel. And the "angels kept not their first estate, but left their own habitation"—Jude 6. Although God was extremely patient with them, he eventually had to call a halt to the rebellion. You know the results of that war in Heaven, for those angels who were cast out are still present in our world today, sometimes in our own homes and hearts.

Well, the justice of God looks rather grim, doesn't it? He didn't spare a city, a nation, a world, or even a universe because of sin! How can this same God ever find enough mercy to pardon one individual sinner?

I'd like to assure you that there is hope for each of us, because God "spared not" one more time. Romans 8:32 tells us that "He **spared not His own Son,** but delivered him up for us all," and if He made this greatest sacrifice, "how shall He not with Him also freely give us all things?"

If you will study the sacrifice of Jesus on the cross, you will discover that this is the greatest time when God "spared not." Here is demonstrated the realization that God gave Himself. None of this idea of God pleading for His Son to go or Jesus pleading with His irate Father to spare these people! Away with such concepts!

Instead, you can see the Father and the Son involved **together** in this great sacrifice. **Both of them** worked for the plan of redemption, and in giving His Son, God gave everything. He gave more than if He could have given Himself. Jesus was the greatest gift that God could have given us. **He spared not His own Son** so that His justice could remain true and His love could equal it.

One day, centuries ago, Jesus was in close conversation with the Father. The angels looked on. The air was heavy with suspense. Everyone was wondering how God's original plan had gone wrong after sin entered, and they were wondering what God would do to complete the plan.

After a long time, Jesus came from that close communion with His Father, and it was revealed that He had offered Himself to die in man's place. So God gave all Heaven, His own Son. He couldn't have given anything more.

Here you see God and Jesus together, one in purpose. And if you like Jesus, then you like God, and if you don't like God, then you don't like Jesus. It's as simple as that. They're **together** in this great plan of redemption.

The cross displays the extent of God's justice: in order to save us, He spared not His own Son.

Study God's character as revealed by Jesus. How did Jesus relate to sinners when He was on this earth?

You see a man coming to the edge of a large crowd down by a lake. He's a leper, considered to be cursed by God. As he comes, people fall back. They don't want him around; they're afraid of being contaminated by this sinner. But Jesus invites this poor leper into His presence, and He touches the untouchable. He says, "They consider you an untouchable under the curse of God. You're supposed to be a great sinner, but I will make you clean." Who was this talking? That was the Father.

You see a woman being dragged through the dust into the presence of Jesus. They stand around ready to heave huge rocks at her to crush her to death. But Jesus says, "I don't condemn you. Go, and sin no more." The perfect balance of justice

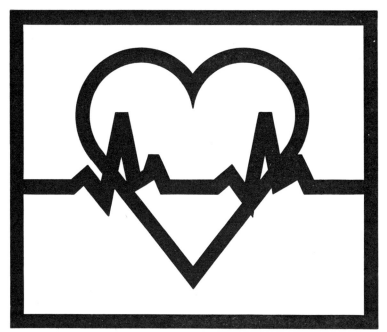

The heart of God the Father beats with the same love for us that His Son, Jesus, showed. He gave us His Son, and now awaits our response to His love.

and mercy in His answer! Who was speaking? It wasn't only Jesus. It was God. The God of the Old Testament? Yes, the same God.

You see a man under the cover of darkness, coming to see Jesus. He doesn't want anyone else to know he's there. And as he tries to enter into a theological debate, he's really saying, "What must I do to be saved? What do I need?"

And Jesus replies, "You must be born again. God so loved the world that He gave His only begotten Son in order to redeem the whole world." The God of the Old Testament? Yes. That's the great God of love—the same yesterday, today, and forever.

You see a man hanging on a cross, and he turns to Jesus and manages to get out of his parched mouth a few words, "Lord, remember me."

And Jesus promises him, "I will remember you. You'll be with Me in Heaven." Who was that? Jesus only? No. That's God, too.

Time and time again He gave the Jews opportunity to repent. They had turned Him down continually, killing the prophets and stoning those who had been sent to help them. Finally He sent His Son Jesus in person, as the greatest manifestation of Himself. "Give them another opportunity." What a demonstration of the glory and mercy of God!

If we had been on the cross, with evil men mocking us, we would have called on the 12 legions of angels to deal with them. But instead, Jesus uttered the pardoning words, "Father, forgive them, for they know not what they do."

Even after the Cross, God's patience wasn't over. After the nation was rejected, He continued to plead with individuals to come to repentance.

The Shekinah glory was removed from the Temple, but God sent the disciples first of all to Jerusalem, the place where Jesus had issued the words of doom, "Your house is left unto you desolate." During all of the missionary journeys of the apostles, the Jewish people were included year after year after year. The early Christian church was not just for the Gentiles. He sent His messengers back repeatedly to "give them more opportunities" to repent, to turn to Him.

As Stephen was stoned to death by an angry mob, the Holy Spirit came upon him, and he prayed, "Forgive them. Don't give up on them yet."

Don't let this story rest simply with the people of Christ's day. His call of mercy and love continues on today, to every person, to every heart. Apply it to your life, to your family, to those you've been praying for, to the drunkard, the dope addict, the seemingly hopeless cases.

Here's a husband who looks good at church, but he fights with his wife at home. What shall we do about him? Leave his case with God. Don't cut him off.

Here's a young person who leads a group in singing gospel songs, but he blasphemes the name of God when he's not up in front. What shall we do with him? Cut him down? No, leave him with God.

Listen, friend, even if you've run away from God because you've misunderstood His character; if you're now tired of run-

The perfect balance of love and justice is displayed in God's gift of His Son: without Jesus He could save none of us, but through Him we all may choose life!

ning, but afraid He won't accept you back, hear His friendly words of invitation, "Come unto me, all ye that labor and are heavy laden, and I will give you rest." Find out what it means to fall low before the cross and to communicate with your Saviour, Lord, and Friend. In His great mercy God has not cut you down. He does not look coldly upon you. He does not turn away with indifference, or leave you to destruction. Looking upon you, He cries, as He cried so many centuries ago concerning Israel, "How shall I give you up?"

Eventually there will come a day when God will no longer spare this world of sin. In the meantime, however, there is redemption for everyone, even for poor people who may appear to have gone past the limit of God's mercy. We have evidence to believe that one reason Jesus hasn't returned yet is for the sake of all who haven't accepted His plan of salvation. His mercy continues. It goes on and on and on.

Then why will God finally bring an end to our world? Does His patience eventually wear out? No. Revelation 11:18 tells us that God's patience is going to continue until man comes to the place of destroying himself.

Even though this world will not be spared, He will spare a group of people, because he spared not His own Son (Malachi 3:17)! Wouldn't you like to be in the group of people that God spares?

How is this possible? How do I respond to His plea?

I have to accept and receive His gift of Christ **each day.** There's no other way, because in order to realize the goodness and mercy of our patient God of justice, I have to continually study and contemplate Him. I may hear about His love from the pulpit or from my Bible class, but this happens only once a week and perhaps even less often. In order to repent daily, I have to contemplate and understand the goodness of God **for my own life** each day. If I neglect this, it has a way of fading from my mind, just as the memory of friends fades when they are absent.

I'm thankful today for a God who loves us enough to send His greatest gift—His Son—to reveal His true character. And He has promised to transform our characters and to give us victory.

What a God we serve! He doesn't treat us the way we treat each other. I'm thankful that God has promised to accept us no matter where we've been or what we've done in the past, that His mercy goes on and on. Shall we not respond in gratitude by getting to know Him, and then by revealing in our own lives to others what He is really like?

Dear Father in Heaven, we thank You for Your patience and mercy in this world of sin. We think of the injustice we've done by misrepresenting Your character of love to others. We don't deserve Your great plan of salvation—we can't do anything to merit it—but we fall in repentance and ask Your forgiveness.

You must be tired of this world of sin and heartache. We would have given up a long time ago, but You con-

Although God, to be just, must eventually destroy this world of sin, He will spare a group of people, among whom we all may choose to be.

tinue to give us more chances. Thank You for sending Jesus on His mission of mercy to reveal that You are our best Friend. Draw us closer to You that we may know You more and more each day, we pray, in Jesus' name, Amen.

7

Working Out Your Own Salvation

Late one afternoon a Christian missionary and a bonze (Buddhist monk) were traveling in the cold mountains of Tibet. Because it was known that no one could survive out on the trail after dark, both travelers were anxious to reach the monastery located some distance ahead. They hurried as fast as they could against the sun, but just as it was nearing dusk, they heard groans coming from below the steep trail.

They looked over the edge of the road, and there they saw a man who had fallen on some rocks below. He couldn't move because of his injuries, and it was obvious that he was in deep trouble.

The bonze gazed down thoughtfully at the injured man and said, "In my religion, we call this a karma. It means that this man was hurt as the result of a cause. Apparently his fate is to die here, but my destination is still ahead of me. I must hurry on to the monastery before it gets dark."

The Christian missionary replied, "This poor, helpless soul is my brother. I can't let him die here. I must go down and try to help him, regardless of what happens to me."

While the bonze hurried on towards the monastery, the missionary made his way down the steep cliff. Finally reaching the place where the injured man was lying, he took off his outer garments and wrapped them around the man, hoisted him to his shoulders, and with great effort finally reached the trail again.

It was getting dark by the time he came within the lights of the monastery, but as he hurried towards this place of refuge, he stumbled over something in the trail. Looking down, he discovered the lifeless body of the bonze who, in the darkness and cold, had already fallen on the trail.

Now, the story sounds melodramatic, and I hesitate to tell it for that reason. Perhaps it's only a parable, but it demonstrates the premise that in trying to save someone else, we save ourselves.

Philippians 2.13 tells us that we must work out our own salvation, and this text has often been misunderstood and misapplied, thus degenerating Christianity into a system of works. However, Jesus told us that some works are involved in the plan of salvation: "Whosoever will come after me, let him deny himself, and take up his cross, and follow me. For whosoever will save his life shall lose it; but whosoever shall lose his life for my sake and the gospel's, the same shall save it"—Mark 8.34, 35.

In order to have a living experience with Christ, we need to do two things. First, we must go to the cross daily with Jesus in order to give up on ourselves and let Him take over. This involves a daily devotional life in which we take significant time alone at the beginning of every day to seek personal acquaintance with Jesus through His Word and through prayer. And if we will seek God with all our hearts, we'll find Him (Jeremiah 29.13).

The other thing we need to do in order to continue and grow in this relationship is another form of communication: involvement in the gospel through the Christian witness and service. And if Philippians 2.13 is applied to Christian outreach, then it is easy to see where the "fear and trembling" comes in! But remember that **God** works in us "both to will and to do His good pleasure."

Now, the person who seeks to become acquainted with God by going out and working for others will save his own life in the process. Often, however, we have had a lot of confusion and misunderstanding as to the purpose and motivation of the Christian witness. The church has always recognized the importance of it, but we've usually relied on man-made approaches to produce the desired results. There have been all sorts of substitutes for the genuine motivation to witness.

Too often we have sought to motivate people toward witnessing by all kinds of awards and devices, advertising the powerlessness of our spiritual lives.

One method we've often used is competition, pitting one group of people against the other. We've resorted to mechanical gimmicks—"initial incentives" such as goals, charts, and other devices which are designed to impress a need upon us. And then we pass out buttons, pins, ribbons, and certificates, with all sorts of rewards and recognition in order to keep everyone working.

I heard about one such device available to churches. It was a board with two sets of lights, one set on each side. In the center the name of the adult Bible school class could be painted. If the class members studied their Bibles every day, they could turn on the lightbulb on one side. If they reached their mission offering goal that week, they could turn on the bulb on the other side. If they were fortunate enough to reach both goals the same week, they could place some tinfoil behind the bulbs to make them glitter.

One week every member of the class, except one who had been away, reached the goals. The other members were very disappointed with the one who had failed. The next week he missed studying his lesson one day; so again they couldn't turn on their lights. The resulting reproof from the rest of the class almost drove him from the church.

Unfortunately, such incidents are all too prevalent. Others have told me of similar experiences with variations of this device. I heard of another place where the lights were turned on at the beginning, and they were turned off if the goals weren't reached!

When we have to resort to these programed methods to get people to read their Bibles, give to missions, or share their faith, we are really advertising to others the stark reality that something is lacking in our own Christian experience. We're announcing the fact that we do not know Jesus as the basis of our Christianity and our salvation. If we really knew Him as a personal Friend, we wouldn't need to be **forced** into study and witnessing.

Another motive we've used for working is the thought of future rewards. We wonder if we've done enough to earn stars in our crowns. We pay very close attention consciously or unconsciously to just how much we've done, keeping track of the "credits" we hope to receive for our work. It's interesting to notice that Israel fell into this same trap. Hosea describes the nation as an "empty vine" that brought forth "fruit unto himself" (Hosea 10:1). What a tragedy when **self** is the primary motive for the work we do!

In 1904 these words of inspiration were penned by a Christian worker: "The Lord is good. He is merciful and tender-hearted. He is acquainted with every one of His children. He knows just what each one of us is doing. He knows just how much credit to give each one. Will you not lay down your credit list and your condemnation list, and leave to God to do His own work? You will be given the crown of glory if you will attend to the work that God has given you"—**Christian Service**, p. 368.

"Well," asks someone, "then what **is** our work?"

In recent years, theologians have debated what constitutes
106

Whenever we base our witness on people's need to receive our "light" in order to be saved, we begin to witness out of guilt or a sense of obligation.

saving knowledge. One group claims that everyone who is ultimately saved in God's kingdom must have had "special revelation" by having heard the specific story of the gospel. Without this, they cannot be saved, and if they are lost, we are responsible. The other group maintains that "general revelation" is enough. People will be saved by what they have done with light, regardless of how small that light may have been. They may be saved even if they never heard of the gospel story. Neither of these views is free from problems.

If everyone is going to be saved or lost according to his acceptance or rejection of the light he has received, then why should the Christian witness at all? This opens the way for a great lack of effort, a passive "rocking chair" type of religion in which we can sit comfortably at home and occupy our minds with great theological and philosophical problems.

On the other hand, those who believe in "special revelation" have the problem of keeping up with the population explosion. Even though we have made great progress in world missions, the world population is growing faster than we are able to spread the gospel. And the "special revelationists" have resorted to appeals to "help others out there." We're supposed to go to the neighbors and the mission fields because of **their** need. Usually our primary motive for giving, telling, and sharing has come from a sense of obligation. Someone with great powers of oratory and persuasion has managed to make us feel guilty for not doing more. He tells us that each year, while we've been sitting there on the church pews doing nothing, millions of human souls are lost for eternity because they haven't heard the gospel. So that afternoon we go out, scared to death. We start ringing doorbells, hoping that no one will answer. Has this ever happened to you?

In the first year of my ministry, I thought people would be eternally saved or lost because of what I did or didn't do. I went out and gave Bible studies. Practically the whole neighborhood attended. But then one night my timing was off and I brought up a controversial point of doctrine before they were ready for it. The next week some of them called and said, "We're going to have company; we can't meet this week." The next week they called and said, "We're going to be away; we have to go out of town." And the following week they said, "Well, let's discontinue the studies altogether."

My reaction was, "Oh, no, there'll be a whole houseful of people who are going to be lost now because of my mistakes." And I'd lie awake at night, looking at the ceiling and worrying about all those people. The only way I could find peace was to conclude, "From now on, I'll give more money to radio and television evangelism; I'll let the experts do my witnessing for me."

Someone came up with another idea that seemed to solve my problem: "I'd rather **see** a sermon than **hear** one any day. If you'll just take a nice loaf of bread to your neighbor, that'll suffice. The Christian has only to be pleasant, good, and kind. Sharing his faith becomes secondary to the way he treats others."

If something has happened to me in relationship to my Lord, I can't keep silent—this spontaneous desire to tell others is true biblical witnessing.

One night I heard a group of physicians discussing this concept of the "strong, silent" witness. All you needed to do was to practice good, clean medicine and sew a good stitch on the incision. The way to witness for Christ was to be an expert in your profession. As they continued to debate this point, a doctor commented, "How far would the gospel have gotten in the days of the apostle Paul if his only witness was to sew a good stitch on his tents?"

On the other hand, what is **our** real reason for witnessing supposed to be? There are two accurate measures of our personal relationship with God: First, who has our thoughts? During the mundane routine of daily living, how often do our thoughts turn to Christ without an outside stimulus? The other indication of our closeness to God is of whom we love to converse. Do we

109

love to tell our friends about Jesus and His love for us?

One afternoon after church I met with a group to discuss the role of the Christian witness in our lives. As we shared our experiences, someone said, "You know, this week God gave us an opportunity to share our faith. It seemed providential that someone ran out of gas in front of our farm. So before we helped him get his car running again, we made him promise to come to church today."

"Oh, did he come?"

"No, he wasn't here. Can't understand why."

If we knew a personal relationship with God, then we would not have to seek promises for church attendance. If we were to study the original intent of the Christian witness, we'd have to scrap most of the gimmicks we've been using. Our synthetic methods have indicated a lack of heart experience with Christ. If we really knew Him, then we'd always have something to share concerning what He means to us, what He has done and is doing for us today. We will witness, not because someone coerced us into it, but because we cannot hold our peace about knowing His presence and goodness in our lives. Then our motivation in doing more for God will be the result of our inward experience with Him instead of outward compulsion from others.

The Bible gives us examples of this genuine, spontaneous outreach to others. There was a lame man who came to Jerusalem to seek the great Healer called Jesus. But when he arrived late one Friday afternoon, he heard about a crucifixion out there on a hill called Golgotha. Weeks went by, and the people who had brought him to Jerusalem went home. There he sat on the Temple steps in despair, begging for something to eat. Two men who had seen their Lord ascend to Heaven passed by—Peter and John. And they said, "We don't have any gold or silver to give, but we'll give you what we have. In the name of Jesus Christ of Nazareth, rise up and walk." And the man jumped to his feet. But that wasn't all—he ran up the steps into the Temple court, and there the authorities finally found him, jumping, leaping, and shouting praises. Praising God for what had happened to him.

If something has happened to me in relationship to my Lord, I can't keep quiet. I don't need a super salesman to force me to get out to witness. I don't need someone to use psychological

God's light is given to us so that we may give it to others, and the more light we share, the brighter our own light will become.

manipulations in order to motivate me.

The lepers and blind men came to Jesus for help, and He healed them. Then He immediately said, "Don't tell anyone what has happened." But it didn't stop them. Instead, they ran and shouted and sang the praises of the One they'd met. I'd like to think that Jesus was merely showing them the impossibility of keeping quiet. This is the whole essence of the Christian witness. If I really know Jesus Christ as my personal Friend, if I know what it means to have meaningful communion with Him each day, I can't keep silent!

When I began in the ministry, I had it all backwards. I thought that if I could succeed in getting the church members involved in outreach, they'd be driven into an experience with Christ. So I found some dynamic personalities to get everybody enthused about witnessing. But the result was that only a very few people were driven to an experience with Christ, while the majority ended up discouraged and frustrated.

In another church, I decided to try a different approach. This time my premise was that no one could possibly be a successful witness for Christ unless he had some sort of experience with Him. How ridiculous it would be to come into a courtroom as a witness if I wasn't at the scene! No one would believe what I'd say unless I have been there myself! So this time I determined to preach revival and reformation and righteousness by faith. I decided to talk about Jesus, encouraging people to study, pray, and seek to become acquainted with God in a personal, one-to-one relationship. And as they responded, I sat back and said, "This is it! When they find that deeper experience with Christ, they'll go out and share with others. I won't have to do anything to prompt them." But then they failed to go out and share with others, and as a result, the revival began to sour. Some of those who had become excited about this experience with Christ ended up worse off than before.

Since then I've met many people who have had problems in their devotional life. Perhaps they realized the significance of learning to know Jesus better and had actually begun the privilege and joy of actual fellowship with Christ through the study of His Word and prayer. But then things began to go wrong, and in nine cases out of 10, the reason was that they didn't share their experience of knowing Christ with others. I really believe this, not only in theory, but in actual practice. I've received letters and I've had people tell me of personal experiences which show that our relationship with Christ cannot grow unless we are involved in outreach for Him.

God is aware of the great principle that when we seek to help others, we are helping ourselves more. That's why, in His great love, He has given us the privilege of working with Him for others as a means of communication with Heaven, as a means of continuing in contact with Heaven. This is one of the facets of the Christian witness that we have overlooked too often.

In order to grow in our relationship with God it is essential to **exercise** by sharing with others what we have received from Him. Activity is the very condition of life, and those who try to remain Christians by passively accepting God's free gifts and

112

There is little support for presenting witnessing only in terms of ringing doorbells at strangers' homes, hitting them with a raft of gospel doctrines.

blessings without going to work for Him are trying to live by eating without exercising. In the physical life, this always results in degeneration and decay. If we refused to exercise our limbs, we would soon lose any power or ability to use them at all.

In the spiritual life the same holds true. If we do not exercise our God-given powers, we not only fail to grow into Christ, but we also lose the strength that we already had. If we are content only to pray and meditate all day without going out to help others, we'll soon cease to pray altogether. On the other hand, God's light is given to us that we may give it to others, and the more we give, the brighter our own will become.

So in the problem of the Christian witness, the only conclusion I've been able to come to is that just as soon as people become excited about knowing Jesus as a personal Friend, then we should also encourage them to witness, and provide every opportunity to get them involved in outreach, sharing, and giving so that their experience with Christ will not die.

Our problem is that we've often presented the idea of witnessing in terms of ringing doorbells at strangers' homes. But what did Jesus say about the Christian witness? In the country of the Gadarenes, Jesus healed a demoniac and cast the evil spirits into a herd of swine. The people were frightened and begged Jesus to leave. The man who had been healed wanted to stay with Jesus, but Jesus told him, "Go home to your **friends** and tell them what the Lord has done for **you**"—Mark 5:19. And this man must have obeyed, because the next time Jesus visited that country, those who had begged Him to leave before now rushed out to welcome Him. They were eager to see Him, because of what this man had told them.

It is true that Jesus told us to "go into all the world and preach the gospel" (Mark 16:15), but there's very little support for the idea that we are supposed to go out "cold turkey" to people we've never seen before and hit them with a raft of gospel doctrines. Instead, I go out to become friends with them, and then I'll be able to tell them what great things the Lord has done for me. What point is there in knocking on doors and ringing doorbells of strangers if I cannot even talk to the person across the aisle of my own church about the love of Jesus?

There is a difference between **our** motivation for witnessing and **God's** for having us do it. **God's** purpose for the Christian witness is to keep us alive in Him. It is not merely to meet the needs of the people "out there," but to meet our own needs. He's not waiting for us to become experts in presenting the programed approach. He's waiting for us to realize that the personal experience with Christ makes all the difference in the world, and for us to realize that becoming actively involved with Him in the work of the gospel is a privilege given by a God of love.

In everyday life, I become acquainted with you by communication: talking to you, listening to you talk to me, and by going places and doing things with you. The same principles operate in the spiritual life: communication. I listen to God through studying His Word, I talk with Him through prayer, and I go places and do things with Him by becoming involved in

God's motive for encouraging Christian witness is to help Christians grow; our motives is to share the happiness we have found in Christ.

the Christian witness.

God knows that as a result of encountering trials and opposition as we witness, not only will we become closer to Jesus, but we will also be driven to our knees with a greater hunger and thirst after righteousness. This will cause us to seek God more and our faith will become strengthened as our experience with Christ grows deeper and richer. It is true that others will also benefit when we become involved in the Christian witness, but God's primary purpose is for our own good.

Then are we supposed to work for God in order to save ourselves? No, that would be a selfish reason for us. **Our** motivation for witnessing is the joy of knowing what a wonderful Friend we have found in Jesus and of wanting to share this happiness with others. Our motivation will be the spontaneous result of having a genuine experience with Christ. And this joy of fellowship with Him is not reserved for just a few. **All** of us can experience it. And as we continue to share what we've received with others, we'll be working out our own salvation by learning to know more and more of Christ.

It happened in a New York hospital that was established to help the alcoholics and those with darker addictions. One night they dragged a man in off the streets for the 50th time.

In the morning the doctor said to him, "Bill, this is the 50th time you've been here."

"Oh, so I'm a half-century plant? Can I have a drink to celebrate the news?"

The doctor replied, "You can forget the comedy. But I'll get you a drink if you'll get out of bed and do a favor for me."

"Oh, hand me my bathrobe!"

The doctor said, "Down the hall is a young fellow who just came in this hospital last night for the first time. All I want you to do is let him have a look at you. You don't have to say a word. Just one look at you might scare him out of ever taking another drink."

So Bill stumbled down the hall and into the room of the younger man. There he stood—bloodshot eyes and matted whiskers. The younger man couldn't miss the message. But then a strange thing happened. Instead of walking away, Bill began to feel sorry for this young victim of alcohol. He said, "You know, there are some people who can't take drink, and you've got to learn in time."

The young man said, "No thanks, I can't."

Bill said, "You must. You've got to believe in a power bigger than yourself."

"I don't believe in a power bigger than myself!"

"Oh, yes, you do!" retorted Bill. "The bottle is bigger than you!" And he continued to talk all morning with this man, and finally when he saw a little response in the young man's heart, he nearly shouted for joy.

The young man asked, "What can I do?"

Bill replied, "Pray. And then let me help you." He was so surprised at his own words that he almost fell over. But he continued to talk with this young man, quoting Bible texts that he had learned in his childhood. Before they left that morning, Bill promised to keep in touch with the young man to encourage him and pray with him.

Bill made many visits to the hospital after that, but never as a patient. Rather, he came as the founder of the worldwide organization known as Alcoholics Anonymous. Its premise is based upon the theory that in trying to help someone else, you always help yourself more.

God knows that's true. He put that principle into operation. And He invites us in His love today to respond to His invitation of getting involved with Him in working for others.

Dear Father in Heaven, we thank You for the privilege You have given us of becoming involved with You in the work of the gospel. Sometimes we have thought it was a chore. Deliver us from relying on all the gimmicks and the programed approach and forgive us for all the things we've tried to do in order to escape from getting involved in outreach. Help us to know You so well that we can't keep still, that we will continue to tell others what You mean to us. We thank You for Your mercy and patience as we learn to know You better. In Jesus' name, Amen.

8

I Give Up What?

When I studied life-saving techniques, the Red Cross instructor taught us some safeguards in trying to rescue a drowning person. He said, "If at all possible, do **not** jump in immediately to save him. Watch him very carefully, but wait until he is about to go under for the traditional 'third time.' When he comes to that point, then plunge in and save him, but not until then."

Why did he caution us to wait? If we were to plunge in immediately, the victim would be struggling. He'd clutch us in a death-like grip, and we both might drown. But if we would wait until he had stopped fighting, then we could safely rescue him.

Did you know that the salvation of man is based upon the same principle? We must come to the place where we are ready to stop fighting the waves of sin. Jesus sees us floundering in the sea of life. We're struggling, desperately trying to fight our sins, trying to overcome our problems. But the devil is stronger and smarter than we are. It doesn't seem we'll ever get victory. Finally, when we have given up and are about ready to sink forever, we admit that we can't make it. We look desperately towards Heaven for help. Only then can Jesus come to rescue us.

You may wonder why God hasn't given you the power to overcome your sins. Perhaps you haven't yet reached the place where you realize your weakness and helplessness. Perhaps you haven't learned what it means to **surrender** to Him.

Most of us realize the importance of "surrender," but we fail to understand exactly **what** and **how** to give up. How easily our attention focuses on the sins and the behavior! We usually think that righteousness is only "right doing" and that the way to do right is to stop sinning (doing wrong).

"Well," says someone, "we have to surrender all our sins and problems before we can be righteous."

So we determine to give up these **things**. Have you ever tried it? One time I became excited about living the victorious Christian life. I promised God that I would surrender my evil habits. To accomplish this, I made a list of seven major sins and resolved to work on them. The first sin on my list was my ugly temper. The next day, I began trying to control my temper. When I'd get angry, I counted to 10. Sometimes I succeeded in not slapping my enemy, but as I counted to 10, my neck was red and the veins stood out, my eyes were bulging, my stomach churned, and my fists were clenched. Somehow this didn't sound like victorious living to me!

Another gimmick I tried was praying at the time of temptation. That's when I discovered something very discouraging: usually by the time I was aware of the temptation, I was so far into it that I either didn't want to pray or there wasn't enough time to pray. It was like writing a check when I didn't have the money in the bank. My prayers for victory didn't work, because I wasn't acquainted with the Source of power.

Someone told me that the real problem was with my thinking. I hadn't learned to control my thinking. And because "as a man thinketh in his heart, so is he," I needed to work on my thoughts. Have you ever tried this one?

"Today I won't think about . . . oops!—I just thought about it!"

Perhaps I'd get too busy to think about it through half of the day. Then I'd stop and say, "Hurrah! Today I haven't thought about—oops! Oh, oh! I just thought about it again!" And my feelings of triumph faded into despair.

Finally I reached the point where I felt I had overcome my temper; so I moved to the next sin on my list. This time I was successful. I found I could get rid of this sin easily, and I became proud of my own abilities. Unfortunately, by the time I started working on #3, I discovered, much to my chagrin, that my bad temper had returned.

**True surrender means abandoning our attempts
to struggle against the waves of sin in our own strength.**

It didn't help my morale when I received a pamphlet describing "One Hundred Sins That Laodicea Must Repent Of." It was discouraging! Is fighting the bad fight of sin the plan that God has for each of us?

Someone else told me, "Look, you don't realize how the victorious life is obtained. Victory comes when you do your part and God does His. You have enough will power to do part of it. You **choose** to be good with your will, then you act with your will power in carrying out your choice. Do the best you can, and God will make up the difference by removing the evil from your heart."

This plan might be termed "subsidy religion," in which God would subsidize my weak power, if I would do my 30%. But I didn't even have the will power to do that much. If I was trying

121

to overcome my temper, I was supposed to make sure that I didn't slap my enemy. Then God would take the hate out of my heart. But my backbone was like wet spaghetti—I couldn't even do my part so that God could take the hate out of my heart. This "subsidy" program kept me frustrated, wondering just how far short I was falling each time.

When I tried harder to conquer my problems, I discovered it to be a fierce and hopeless battle. If I had any time left over after fighting my sins, then I'd read a verse or say a prayer to keep God happy, but usually after hassling all of my problems, I didn't have enough time or energy to bother.

I found that it was possible to fight the devil so hard that I became more like him. It reminded me of my efforts to go to sleep at night. Someone told me that if I couldn't sleep, I was supposed to start relaxing my fingernails, then my toes, my hands and feet, and so on, until I relaxed everything I owned, and I would finally become so relaxed that I would automatically go to sleep. But as I tried it, the more tense I got, and I ended up being more wide awake than ever.

What's the problem of a neurotic? Everyone has problems, but the neurotic's biggest problem is his eternal concern with his problems. As he looks at them and concentrates on them, they grow bigger and bigger, until they're too big to handle. It's possible to be a spiritual neurotic, too.

As I became more and more discouraged, I began wondering what surrender was really all about. What did it mean to surrender, anyway? I searched the Bible to find out exactly what God requires of us.

Romans 9:30, 31 describes two groups of people, the Jews and the Gentiles. The Jews were too concerned with their own goodness and righteousness in keeping the law through their own strength, and they failed to recognize Jesus when He walked among them. Their attention was fastened on themselves. On the other hand, the Gentiles were acknowledged sinners who were able to see Jesus Christ as the Son of God, and they came and bowed humbly at His feet. What made the difference? The Jews were fighting the fight of sin. They had neither the time nor energy left for God. The Gentiles were free to fight the fight of faith. Do you see the difference?

No wonder Jesus said, "I came not to call the righteous, but sinners to repentance!" It's true that all of us are sinners, but
122

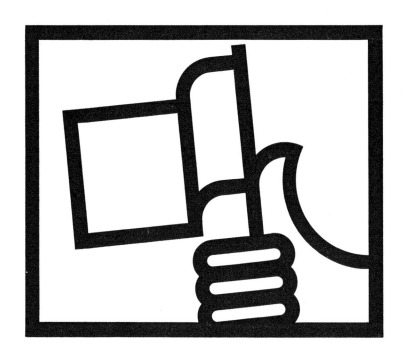

**Not until we give up the bad fight of sin can
God give us victory in the good fight of faith.**

Jesus was reminding us that some do not realize their sinful condition and their need of a Saviour to empower them to overcome.

Christians usually think that there are two battlefronts: the bad fight of sin and the good fight of faith, and we often try to fight both at the same time. Is this what God wants us to do?

The apostle Paul tells us that "to him that worketh is the reward not reckoned of grace, but of debt. But to him that worketh not, but believeth on him that justifieth the ungodly, his faith is counted for righteousness"—Romans 4:4, 5. Notice that our effort is that which is necessary to **believe**. This holds true for both justification and sanctification, because sanctification is simply moment-by-moment justification.

"Wait!" objects someone. "You're describing 'cheap grace,

but the Bible says that we have to **fight**."

True. But **how** do I fight the devil? He's stronger than I am. This text suggests that for the one who does not work on the bad fight of sin, but lets God fight for him (the fight of faith), his **faith** is counted for righteousness. The only way to resist the devil is to turn the battle over to superior forces. The good fight of faith is the effort to know God and Jesus Christ whom He has sent. The Bible terms it a fight, because the devil will battle every inch of the way to keep us from knowing Jesus. He knows that if people accept this truth fully, his power will be broken.

The reason we've become so discouraged in trying to live the Christian life is that we've never known **how** to overcome. We often talk about what we should do, but people say, "Yes, I've tried that, and it doesn't work."

Eventually the follower of Christ must give up trying to "do what is right" in his own power. He gives up on the idea that he can do anything about his life, except to go to God, because surrender has primarily to do with **self**, not sins.

When I determined to surrender my seven sins, I was actually a long way from it. In fact, when I was fighting my faults, weaknesses, and problems, I was doing just the opposite of genuine surrender.

"Well," says someone, "then what is surrender?"

Surrender means giving up the idea that we can do anything at all except come to Christ and seek a daily relationship with Him. It means giving up the idea that we can do anything about our sins apart from Christ. Sin is stronger than man's will power, whether he is strong or whether he is weak. It is useless for **us** to fight it. We must surrender **ourselves!** That's what Jesus meant when He invited us to "Come unto Me, and I will give you rest"; He was appealing for us to give up the bad fight of sin and take up the good fight of faith instead.

VE-Day and VJ-Day came, bringing an end to World War II. The Axis forces had been brought to surrender. What did they surrender? Did they say, "We give up all of our submarines?" No. Did they say, "We'll give up our tanks and our guns?" No. They gave up themselves and their fighting, and that automatically took care of the tanks, the planes, the submarines, the bombs, the guns, and the whole business. Our problem in Korea, Vietnam, and other places around the world is that we have talked truce, cease-fire, and summit con-

**By putting ourselves totally in God's hands,
we lay hold of the victory Jesus has already obtained.**

ferences, but never **surrender.**

We have to surrender the idea that we can attain righteousness apart from Jesus! The devil likes to have us work on our righteousness as a substitute for knowing Jesus. And it is possible for some to give up their evil tempers as an escape from giving up themselves to **God**! This is a dead-end street, because the strong who are able to do right externally become proud, while the weak who are only able to fail miserably become discouraged.

Righteousness has to be defined in terms of something more than right doing! I've found only one satisfactory definition for the ultimate of righteousness, and it's found in a person. Jeremiah 23:6 tells us that **Christ** is our righteousness. Righteousness must **never** be separated from Jesus Christ, and it is a **gift** that we can only receive when we come to Him. If we seek it apart from Him, we will never find it, for righteousness comes only to those who seek Jesus instead.

Usually we think that sin, being the opposite of righteousness, is "wrong doing," but if righteousness is Jesus, then sin becomes separation from Him. **Sin is doing or being anything, regardless how good or bad it may be, apart from the faith relationship with Christ** (Romans 14:23).

If the lack of relationship with Christ is the key to sin, then both weak and strong qualify. We're all equally sinners, not because of what we've done, but because of what we are. And the knowledge of what you are is necessary before you can meaningfully come to Christ in surrender.

When I was a little boy of 3' 9", I wanted to be six feet tall. I began hanging on the clothesline post in order to get taller. But when I'd go in to measure myself against a six-foot mark on the wall, I was still only 3' 9". If I had taken up all of my time with hanging on the clothesline without ever taking time to eat, I would never have become six feet tall. I probably would have been six feet under!

How do I grow physically? Do I work on the growing? Or do I work on my eating and discover that I will grow naturally as a result? If I work on the growing, I'll never make it.

But isn't this what we've usually done in our Christian experience? We know what we should be like, and we often work on trying to be like that. Instead, we should work on the cause of the goodness—the relationship. If my sins are the result of separation from God, then I should seek to maintain the close communion with God, and He will take care of my sins.

Our part in continuing salvation is to abide in Him. We are not able to save ourselves, but Christ fights our battles for us and gives us the victory (John 14:4, 5; I Corinthians 15:57).

The Bible is full of promises by which we can become victorious (II Peter 1:4).

Ephesians 2:8, 9: "For by grace are you saved through **faith**, and **that** not of yourselves. **It is the gift of God.** Not of works, lest any man should boast." Salvation and faith are **gifts.**

I Thessalonians 5:23, 24: "I pray God your whole body and soul and spirit be preserved blameless unto the coming of our Lord. Faithful is He who calls you, and He also will do it." Do what? He'll preserve you blameless.
126

The character of true surrender involves focusing our attention on Jesus, rather than on our own performance.

John 16:33: "Be of good cheer. I have overcome the world." Christ has already won the victory, and our part is to accept His gift.

Jude 24: "Now unto Him that is able to keep you from falling, and to present you faultless." Sanctification is also God's work.

II Peter 2:9: "The Lord knows how to deliver the godly out of temptation." I become godly by getting in touch with the One who is godly!

Promises, promises. The Bible is full of promises, assuring us that God will fight our battles and win for us. But our actions often say that He isn't big enough to keep His promises. I've got to do something myself; I've got to count to 10; I've got to control my thoughts. And invariably my attention is focused back on self.

We should **not** look at ourselves, for the more we dwell upon our own imperfections, the less strength we shall have to overcome them. Each one will have a close struggle to overcome sin in his own way. This is at times a very painful and discouraging work, because as we see the deformities in our character we keep looking at them when we should look to Jesus and put on the robe of His righteousness. Everyone who enters the pearly gates of the City of God will enter as a conqueror, and his greatest conquest will have been the conquest of **self**.

Then what is the solution? I'm inviting you today, my friend, to break from the self-centered and the sin-centered life. I'm inviting you to look away from your problems and to look instead to your Saviour, the Lord Jesus Christ. Does that sound like good news to you?

"Well," says someone, "then how do I get over my problems?"

Accept the fact that you can do nothing apart from Christ (John 15:5). This text doesn't say that you can do 90% or 30% apart from Him, because it is talking about man's inner nature, where all are equally helpless. We can do **nothing** apart from Christ.

On the other hand, I can do **everything** through Christ (Philippians 4:13), and if this is true, then the only thing to do is to get in touch with Him and keep in touch with Him. And the devil will do all he can to keep me away from Christ.

If I want to give up my temper, I don't try working on my temper. I don't even pray overly much about it, because it is possible, even in my prayers, to fight the bad fight of sin: "Lord, help me today not to do this, and this, and this." My attention is then on myself or things!

Instead, I focus the attention on my **relationship**—on **Him!**—and pray, "Lord, help me today to realize Your presence and power. You've promised it. And if I can't have You in my life, I'm dead. Won't You come in and take over? Take control of my life for today."

I choose **Christ**, and use my will power to seek Him, and as I learn to do this He takes care of my temper for me. In order to get rid of any problem, I have to get in touch with the only One who has the power! But often we don't allow Christ to come in until we are tired and worn out with battling the evil forces

128

ourselves.

Once when I was pastoring in Sacramento, the phone rang at two o'clock in the morning. I stumbled down the hall, and a woman's voice on the other end of the line said, "Sir, can you help me? I need help!"

I said, "What kind of help do you need at this time of the night?"

She replied, "I need God. Sir, do you know God?"

Now, how would you reply to that? I've thought since then about all of the inadequate answers I could have given instead. I could have told her that I was a preacher, that my father, uncle, and brother were also preachers, that I had the ribbons to prove I studied my Bible class lesson faithfully, and that I faithfully succeeded in raising my mission goal each year. But would these have been adequate answers? No, she wanted to know **God!**

I'd just been developing the concept in my own thinking about God's promise to fight for us if we'd only seek Him, but I was wondering if it was really that simple. And then God gave me Alice, this woman, for a test case.

Alice was a high-class alcoholic. Intelligent and educated, she lived in a clean apartment. But alcohol had gotten the best of her. It seemed hopeless. She had tried everything possible, but finally was about to take sleeping pills to end her life. She'd taken half of them when she panicked and called the nearest preacher she could find from the telephone book. It happened to be me. I'd never met her before, but she got right to the heart of the problem. She said, "I need to know God. Can you help?"

She had finally gotten to the point of surrender, because she had given up on the idea that she could do anything at all except go to God just as she was. She knew nothing about Him, but now she felt a need of Him.

So she asked me, "Do you know God?"

After a long pause, I said, "I believe I know Him, and I would like to know Him better. I'd like to help you find Him, too."

She excused herself from the phone to get rid of the pills she had taken. After she had sent them down the drain, she came back and we talked for three hours about knowing God. I talked to her only about the love of God and the power of Jesus Christ and told how she, a poor helpless alcoholic, could become acquainted with Him. I assured her that He would accept her just as she was and would change her life for her.

The next day we talked for five more hours about only that one point—the necessity of knowing God as a personal Friend. Finally, at the end of those eight hours, she prayed a personal prayer, asking God to accept her as she was and expressing a desire to know Him better.

Now, according to the usual procedure, the wise thing for me to do would have been to remove all the alcohol from her cupboard. And I would have gone home that night with a pocket full of bottles. Instead, I decided to let God take care of that. I'd seen too many people toss away their cigarettes, only to go to the store a little later and buy a new pack. So I left the bottles where they were.

Little by little, I taught her how to maintain her own personal, daily connection with Christ. While we were teaching her to know God day by day, she slipped once and felt terrible—**not** because of her inability to cope with alcohol, but because she had disappointed God. And as she continued to seek God, His power was realized in a wonderful way. Because of her absolute surrender, her longing for drink left her completely.

Why was this possible? Because she had admitted her sin and given up on herself, and God could help her when she came to that point.

Perhaps our problems aren't as noticeable as Alice's, but the principle remains the same. We cannot do anything ourselves apart from Christ. Yet we often hinder His power to help us by getting in the way.

You see, there are two ways to fight God. There's the atheistic way in which the person says, "I'm against God. In fact, I'm not even sure He exists; I'm fighting the idea that He cares about us and is active in our world."

The more subtle way is getting involved in His work, His business, trying to get His job done yourself.

It's like fighting the auto mechanic. I can fight him by advertising that I don't believe in auto mechanics. I refuse to take my car to him.

A more subtle way is for me to take my car to the garage. The mechanic opens up the hood, but as he does this, I poke my head in from the other side and say, "Now, be careful. This is a very delicate engine."

Surrender is not a one-time, emotional event; it is the natural outgrowth of a daily communion with God.

And as he starts working, I say, "No, don't touch the fan belt. I just put on a new one. And stay away from those new spark plugs. Keep your grubby little hands off the carburetor, because it's very delicate, too."

I can continue to harass the poor mechanic until he throws down his tools, throws up his hands, and says, "All right. I give up. Take your car and repair it yourself."

God can only deliver us by taking over our battles for us. And we cannot receive His help unless we recognize that we are powerless to do anything in our own strength. Paul says, "I am crucified with Christ; nevertheless I live." What is he saying? He is saying that his strength is made perfect in weakness and death, for when he is weak, then he is strong in Christ (II Corinthians 12:9, 10).

The whole essence of Christ's message was self-surrender, and the strong-willed Pharisees didn't like His message. They said, "We don't need this man alive," because He toppled their sand castles and undermined their false security. But the weak people gathered around Him, because they loved to be in His powerful presence.

The challenge of the gospel today is for us to face the enigma that we must become weak no matter how strong we are. God is waiting for us to realize that we're sinners having nothing to offer. He's longing for each of us to come to Him just as we are and confess, "God, I can't do it. I've been able to accomplish everything else but this. I do need You. I'll always be a sinner, and if You want me to live victoriously, You'll have to do it **all** for me."

Only then can the Lord step in and save us. If you have never realized God's power in your life, it is very probable that you have never completely realized your helplessness.

What is the answer—the way in which we leave the bad fight of sin and take up the good fight of faith? It is the private, devotional life of the individual. Spending time alone **every day** with God in personal, individual communication with Him is the way that we live in touch with Him. If you do not spend this time with Him, regardless of how good you are, you're powerless. And Christ cannot be the center of your life unless you keep in touch with Him **each day**.

One time I gave an anonymous, one-question quiz to high-school students: "When you get to Heaven, what will be the first thing you'll do?"

As I read over the various answers, they strangely fell into a similar category: "When I get to Heaven, I'd like to see who else got there"; "I'd like to see who didn't get there"; "I'd be so surprised I don't know what I'd do"; "I'd like to ride a lion"; "I'd like to see my house"; "I'd like to start asking questions." And on and on and on.

My heart was sinking, until I came to one that I'd been hoping to see: "When I get to Heaven, the first thing I want to do is to cast myself at the feet of Jesus and thank Him for making it possible for me to be there."

If Jesus Christ is not the center of your life right now, He won't be the center of your life if you get to Heaven.

In God's Word we meet a loving Father we can trust, and into whose hands we can surrender our lives.

I went to my church and took an anonymous survey of several hundred members, trying to see if they were spending any time at all in seeking Jesus. I discovered that only one out of four was doing this, and that meant that 75% of my congregation was trying to be good enough to be saved—to live a moral life—apart from God.

My appeal to you is to seek this personal acquaintance with Jesus Christ. I'm talking to you, my friend, particularly if you're an impossible case, if you've tried everything and are now bitter. Please, there's something available for you that you haven't understood yet. Often when someone gives up religion and becomes a bad sinner, if he only knew it, he was nearly at the point of genuine surrender, because God takes people who give up on themselves. When you're at the end of your rope, then you're the closest to God, and all you need to do is fight the good fight of faith by seeking Jesus.

The principle and premise of the great theme of righteousness by faith is that as Christ comes into the life, sin is crowded out by Him. It is not stamped out by us.

This great concept has been humorously described by Robert Service, the poet laureate of Alaska. He tells the story of a preacher who went to Alaska as a missionary. One night he got lost in a blizzard and nearly died. His rescuer was Bill, a degenerate reprobate who smoked 40 cigarettes per day. Bill dragged the missionary back to his cabin, which was several miles away. The storm was so severe that they were snowed in for days, trying to keep warm.

Days and nights went by. They were bored. The preacher found solace in reading his Bible, but the only thing Bill could do was smoke. One day he ran out of magazine pages, which he'd been using to roll his cigarettes. As he saw the preacher reading his Bible, he got a bright idea.

He said, "Please, give me some pages from your Bible so I can roll some more cigarettes. I'm going out of my mind! I'm desperate!"

The preacher was aghast: "Never!"

"But I saved your life!"

"Never!"

Bill threatened and pleaded, but the preacher refused to yield. Another day passed, and in the middle of the night, the preacher was awakened by Bill, who in final desperation had brewed a cup of deadly strychnine and was ready to drink it: "I've had it. Good-bye! ..."

The preacher said, "Wait! I've got an idea. I'll give you pages from my Bible if you promise to read every page before you smoke it."

According to this poem, Bill smoked from Genesis to Job, but then something peculiar happened. He read more and more, but smoked less and less. Finally he conceded, "Here, take your Bible back. Guess I've had enough. Your paper makes a mighty rotten smoke."

What was the basic principle again? If you have problems, seek Christ instead of concentrating on your problems. I don't fight the bad fight of sin; I give that up and seek Christ instead. God has promised to fight for us; He's already gained the victory, and it's ours as a gift if we accept Him. Our fight is to seek Him!

What do I give up when I surrender to Him? I give up **myself and my independence.** No wonder the battle with self is called the greatest battle ever fought! Will you join me in seeking to know God **each day**?

> As children bring their broken toys
>   With tears for us to mend,
> I brought my broken dreams to God
>   Because He was my Friend.
>
> But then instead of leaving Him
>   In peace to work alone,
> I stayed around and tried to help
>   Through ways that were my own.
>
> At last I snatched them back and cried,
>   "How can You be so slow?"
> "My child," He said, "what could I do?
>   You never did let go."

Dear Father in Heaven, You are strong; we are weak, even though we haven't realized it. We know there's no hope apart from You. Forgive us for thinking that we had the power and for depending on ourselves. Please teach all of us to fight the fight of faith by letting You take over our battles for us. And please help us to know You as our Friend—in a deeper and deeper way, not just tomorrow, but every day until Jesus comes. We ask in His name, Amen.

9

Doing Worse
When We Try

Sometimes I've heard Christians say, "What's wrong with my Christian experience? When I've tried to spend time each day getting acquainted with Jesus, then the rest of the day has been horrible! I've found myself with more problems, committing more sins, than I ever did before I became a Christian. Why doesn't it really work for me? Wasn't I really converted?"

Does this sound familiar? Have you found it true in your own experience? Often when a person dedicates his life to Christ, he has the impression that all his problems will be solved once and for all. Perhaps he has listened to success stories of others, and thus he becomes discouraged when his own failures **increase**.

While it sounds sacrilegious to say that we often live worse when we pray than when we don't pray, many have discovered this experience to be a reality in their own lives. The enigma of experiencing worse lives in terms of performance and behavior when a person prays has caused many to cease continuing to seek the deeper life with Christ. Because I've been asked this question again and again by frustrated Christians, I believe it is important to understand why things do not necessarily immediately improve after we come to Christ.

To understand the answer to this question, we'll have to take a look at the greater scene—the controversy between good and evil, and when we see what occurs and why it is allowed, perhaps we'll know better why things often go worse when we pray.

One man experienced this in his life thousands of years ago, and an entire book of the Bible is dedicated to this case history: Job.

One day the members of the court of Heaven assembled in the presence of the Lord. Satan was there among them, representing our world, and when the Lord asked him where he had been, he replied, "Ranging over the earth from end to end. In fact, I'm in charge down there. Everyone is following **me**!"

The Lord asked him, "Are you sure **everyone** is following you? You must have overlooked my servant Job. He's a special person on the earth, for he has a blameless and upright life, respects Me, and refuses to do wrong."

Satan answered, "Well, he has good reason to serve You. After all, You've completely surrounded him with protection. Look at his family and all his possessions! Whatever he does You have blessed, and his herds have increased beyond measure. No wonder he worships You! But how deep does his loyalty really go? If You do not continue to bless him with all those material possessions, will he still serve You? If You stretch out Your hand and remove all that he has, he'll curse You to Your face."

The discussion went on, and finally Satan said, "You claim to be just and fair. If You'll accept my challenge, I'll **prove** his love for You to be only apparent and worthless."

Now, God didn't have to accept the devil's challenge. In fact, He never had to permit the devil to continue living after he introduced sin into the universe. But because of His great plan of redemption, in which **we choose** which side we're going to follow, God had to accept the devil's challenge.

He replied, "So be it. You can have freedom to do anything you like with his possessions. The only restriction is that you don't touch Job himself."

The devil agreed to the terms and immediately left the Lord's presence to begin his evil work. In quick succession, tragedies fell upon Job. The Sabeans stole his thousand yoke of cattle and killed the servants; fire destroyed his 7,000 sheep, and three bands of Chaldeans took his 3,000 camels. The worst blow came when his 10 children were killed during a celebration in their eldest brother's house. In fact, Job lost everything except his wife. Perhaps, as you will see by her future actions,

Many sincere Christians ask:
"When I'm trying to be God's person
—but the roof falls in—in terms of my performance—
does that mean I was never really converted?"

she should have been the first to go! Anyway, Job did not curse God or blame Him for the disasters that came upon him.

Satan returned to the next council meeting with the members of the court of Heaven. They took their places in God's presence, and God asked the devil about his recent activities.

Satan replied, "Oh, I've been ranging over the earth from end to end, collecting more and more people to my side!"

God reminded him, "Well, at least one person has not turned from allegiance to Me. My servant Job is blameless and upright. He avoids all manner of evil, because he loves Me. You incited Me to ruin him without cause, but his integrity is still unshaken. You lost the challenge, and it proves that Job still has the proper motive for serving Me."

But Satan was unwilling to concede defeat yet. He immediately made new demands for testing God's fairness: "There's nothing a man will grudge to save himself. Skin for skin! Your test wasn't fair, because You didn't allow me to touch him. If You will stretch out Your hand and touch his bones and flesh, then he'll curse You to Your face!"

God replied, "So be it. He's in your hands. You can do anything you want to, but you must spare his life."

The devil left God's presence and smote Job from head to foot with boils. Job was forced to sit outside on a heap of ashes, trying in vain to get rid of his miseries. At this point, Mrs. Job remarked, "Do you still persist in thinking that God is going to protect you? It does seem that He's deserted you. Is it still worth serving Him? Why don't you curse Him and die? Then all your troubles will be over."

When she spoke those words, the devil probably smiled, for he had succeeded in making her blame God for all misfortunes and hardships. He remarked to his compatriots, "Now we've got his wife on our side. Just a matter of time, and we'll have Job, too. We can't fail! Success is on its way!"

When the test had ended for Job, however, his integrity remained unshaken, for he refused to curse God, and as a result, God was able to restore double possessions to him, without further question or challenge from the devil.

Have you ever wondered why God allowed the devil to challenge His justice? Why did He permit the devil to dare Him in this manner? It almost seems that He didn't have enough power to take care of His own people.

Of course, God is big enough to protect His own, and the devil knows that. His constant attack is to see whether or not those who claim to follow Christ are genuine disciples: "You think this person really loves You? Not so! He only comes because he can get things from You. I'll prove it if You'll give me the chance."

And God replies, "Go ahead. Try to prove it if you can."

Why does God agree? In the great plan of salvation, He has pledged never to overstep Himself until the issues in the whole controversy are clear beyond the shadow of a doubt to the universe. He voluntarily limits His power in proportion to the options He gives to the devil. In the closing scenes of this world's history, even though it will seem apparent that God is letting the world run completely out of control by leaving Satan in charge, He will also have freedom to pour out His power, strength, and Holy Spirit in greater measure, matching good with evil in its impact on a world of sin.

Somewhere in this controversy between good and evil, between Christ and Satan, we become involved, because the prince of evil contests **every inch** of ground over which God's people advance in their journey toward the heavenly city.

"Well," asks someone, "if the war is between Christ and Satan, then how am I supposed to fit into the picture?"

The book **Education** suggests that we are very much involved:

> (The Bible student) should gain a knowledge of ... God's original purpose for the world, of the rise of the great controversy, and of the work of redemption. He should understand the nature of the two principles that are contending for supremacy .... **He should see how this controversy enters into every phase of human experience;** how in every act of life he himself reveals the one or the other of the two antagonistic motives; and how, whether he will or not, he is even now deciding upon which side of the controversy he will be found (p. 190).

In other words, this same conflict that raged over the life of Job is going on in every person's experience. It may not be too noticeable to the Laodicean, however, because the devil finds lukewarmness—being neither concerned with that which is hot nor that which is cold—quite acceptable to his whole program.

If you are still operating on the level of "Jesus loves me, this I know" and have never searched for a deeper fellowship and a personal encounter of communion with God, then you probably have never been troubled with having things go worse when you pray. This subject could be highly irrelevant to right now. But if you should ever decide to seek a personal acquaintance with God that goes deeper than mere formality, that is more than just going to church and appearing religious, then be prepared for this experience in your life. Perhaps if you understand the overall picture, you'll keep your courage when this happens.

"Well," you say, "what exactly happens when I take up the good fight of faith by trying to seek God to know Him as my Friend?"

Basically, this is what happens: First, you wake up to the realization that salvation and the deeper Christian life are not based upon performance or externals. They are based only upon **relationship** with God. This breakthrough is the first step away from being a **status quo** lukewarm Christian, and it may take years before it is fully understood in experience. After attempting to teach this important concept to students, I've had to conclude that only the Holy Spirit can succeed in convicting a person of his need to know God personally.

The problem is that we're cripplingly hooked on this tendency to measure our Christian experience and salvation by our performance. And even after we begin to seek the deeper life of relationship, we are still addicted to the habit of measuring our success according to our behavior.

Now, please don't think that I'm doing away with good behavior. I'm not saying that you should go out and do exactly as you please, regardless of rules and regulations. Behavior **is** important, not as a cause of our salvation, but as the **result** of becoming acquainted with God.

"Wait!" objects someone. "If my behavior is supposed to improve when I get acquainted with God through His Word and through prayer, then why is my behavior worse than ever when I try this method? That doesn't make sense!"

Again, you're measuring your Christian experience and closeness to God by your performance and actions. **But Christianity is based upon whom you know, not what you do as you're learning to know Him better.** Your part in the great plan of God is to become acquainted with Him, and your behavior is His concern.

Now, after I realize that I must know God personally, I begin to wish for this deeper experience with Him. All other godly people seem to know Him as their Friend; so I begin seeking Him. But then everything goes wrong.

Often on the days that I know He has heard me, when I know that my prayers went higher than the ceiling—on the days that I have found meaningful communication with Him and an actual sense of His presence—the roof caves in.

**When God accepted Satan's challenge over the sincerity
of mankind's love, He put His name on the line,
depending on us to validate His character
and the impact of His love.**

At this point, if I don't understand the great conflict between good and evil, if I can't see beyond my own immediate crisis to realize why I'm doing worse when I pray, then I'll conclude at the end of the day, "Well, I guess **that** didn't work! Seeking God certainly didn't do anything for me today. I did worse than I've ever done before! This devotional time in which I seek God can't be the solution to my problems. It doesn't work; so I'll sleep in tomorrow morning."

The next morning, I skip my devotions, and then, sure enough, I have a good day. I live a perfect life—no losing my temper, yelling at the children, or becoming impatient at work. No sins, no problems. It's a good day.

The obvious conclusion, of course, is: "Well, I guess this proves it. This deeper life they talk about is not that important, because

I had a better day when I didn't spend time with God!"

I might decide that in order to get over my problems, I must fight the fight of sin instead of faith, and I clap myself on the back over any apparent success, not knowing that the evil one who was responsible for **both** days is clapping me on the back, too.

If this sounds like something out of **Screwtape Letters,** then I apologize to C. S. Lewis. But this experience of having more problems when I cease fighting my sins and seek God instead can continue **ad infinitum** for the poor Christian who doesn't understand the overall controversy. And he can only understand it when he realizes that the experience of Job is being repeated in his life.

Now let's look at this same situation from the bigger scene. The devil sees that I am becoming uneasy with my **status quo** religion, because the Holy Spirit is getting through to me with the realization that I need to know God personally. And when the devil sees me going to my knees before God's open Word, seeking the deeper life with God, his enemy, he immediately calls a "Ways and Means" committee of his imps to prevent me from "keeping on keeping on."

Once his plans are laid, he shakes his fist at God and accuses: "You think he loves You? How deluded can You be? He's not seeking You because of love. He only thinks he'll get more things from You—solutions to his problems and the promise of an eternity of riches. Right now, he thanks You for all Your blessings, but if You'll remove them, he'll cease to seek You."

This is the devil's challenge—the same that took place in the experience of Job—and now the controversy is between God and the devil. Of course, God could easily banish the devil, just as He could have annihilated him in the beginning. But God has chosen not to do that, even though He has the power. Whenever the devil makes an accusation against the justice of God, then God says, "All right, so be it. Prove your point."

The devil says, "I can't prove it unless You let me at him." "Okay," God says, "you have My permission."

So the next day, when the devil sees me seeking God again, he and his imps move in on me with all their machine guns blazing. Everything goes wrong. I live worse than I ever have before. And at the close of the day, I am left to cast a deciding

Job showed us the path to true spiritual victory: he trusted God; in spite of all his suffering, he never turned from leaving his case in God's hands.

vote between the two contending forces in the universe. Is God right in saying that I love to fellowship with Him? Or is the devil right in saying that I am using God in order to get things from Him?

If I don't understand this underlying conflict, then I'll say, "Forget it, God. You certainly didn't help me out at all today. Look at what happened when I tried to seek the deeper life with You. You can have it for Yourself!"

And so I have cast my vote on the enemy's side. When he sees me neglecting this special time alone with God, the devil and his imps have a celebration in the regions where they dwell, and they laugh at God's claims to love and justice.

When their "Ways and Means" committee meets again, what do you suppose they decide to do? It doesn't take much brains to figure it out. They see that by giving me a bad day, I've decided to stop spending time alone with God. What would you do the next day if you were the devil? The committee discusses the situation and concludes, "See, we've succeeded! He's not seeking God today. Let's stay away from him. Give him a good day!"

Then, the next day, everything goes fine. I'll say, "See! This proves it. I live a better life when I don't spend the time with God!"

And the devil can go back to God in triumph and say, "Your claims are false! He only wanted to get things from You, and when he discovered that I could do more for him, he turned to me! Oh, he might remain in Your church; he might even try to obey Your laws by himself, but both You and I will know that he's really on **my** side now! I've won!"

Aren't these the kind of forces we are battling in our world today? Subtle? Yes. Effective? Yes. Strange as it may seem, a person can continue this process for weeks and perhaps even years. Have you found this to be true in your own experience? It has certainly happened in mine. I lived "on-again, off-again, on-again, off-again" in terms of seeking God, without ever realizing what was going on. It proved to me that there was a devil in the universe, because I had plenty of personal confrontations with him! For a long time, I was mad at God, because He allowed the devil to move in on me, even though I was trying to spend time with God. But the longer I looked at the whole scene, the more I began to see God's great love in the process.

When I finally am able to realize that this is "Job II" in my own life, then something like this takes place. I think, "Isn't that interesting? **Why** am I seeking God anyway? If I love Him and enjoy the fellowship and communication with Him, then shouldn't I continue to seek Him, regardless of how the day has gone? If everything goes wrong, that's immaterial. I'll still continue to seek Him, because I love to be with Him."

If I get to this point, however, the devil moves in with another insinuation: "You can't go back to God tomorrow morning, because you've done everything wrong today! God won't accept you for fellowship until you get rid of your sins!"

Sometimes he succeeds in making me think that I have to become more righteous before I can come back— that I must generate repentance and develop a good motive for coming
146

By choosing to continue a devotional relationship with God—even when our performance "slips"—we demonstrate the dynamics of a life of faith.

before He will listen to me again.

Is this the way God operates? Let me ask you something: How do I ever get rid of my sins? How do I ever experience genuine repentance?

This may sound like sacrilege to the behavior-minded person, but I'd like to remind you that I cannot experience repentance or receive God's power to overcome my sins by staying away from Him. Even if I have done everything wrong today, I should go back to Him immediately. The behaviorist would say, "Well, I'd better wait until I've chalked up at least 14 days of good conduct in order to appease Him and show Him I'm sorry. **Then** I'll come to Him and He'll accept me."

No, that's a dead-end street! It always has been and always will be. It won't help me to stay away from God, because my only hope for victory is in Him. Even if I have spent time with Him in the morning, only to lose my temper during the day, fight with my wife, yell at the children, blow up at my boss (and thereby lose my job), and get drunk, I must return **immediately** for communication with Him.

And I say to God, "Father, things certainly went bad today. But I'm coming back to You because I need to know You better. I **want** to know You better. I'd like to learn to love You for the right reasons. Please teach me to continue in fellowship with You regardless of what happens."

When I shift gears from behaviorism to fellowship and relationship with God, then and only then does it become possible for me to continue seeking Him constantly. Then and only then can God give victory and do things for me that He wasn't able to do before. I'll decide, "I'm going to seek God for His sake, not for what He can do for me now or in the future, but because of what He has already accomplished for me through the Cross. I'm going to seek Him, not so I can get to Heaven or get victory over my sins, but because I'm grateful for His gift of His Son."

It's not easy to get the right motive for seeking God; in fact, we have to pray for it. We need God's help even for this because our initial motive is always selfish. There's no question about it—it's selfish. But if I continue seeking Him consistently, instead of "on-again, off-again," then God is able to help me.

If I choose to follow Him regardless of what happens, the scene changes when God and the devil meet again.

God says, "Where have you been?"

"Oh, I've been ranging to and fro on the earth, going from one end to the other. I've succeeded in getting more people to follow me. They've proved You wrong!"

"Wait a minute! I still have followers on earth. Have you considered my servant? He has remained faithful to Me."

Satan replies, "Well, I've been working on him with everything I have."

God says, "I know. I've been watching. But in spite of everything you've done to turn him against Me, he is still seeking fellowship and communication with Heaven, isn't he?"

And right there the devil gets nervous and begins kicking his feet in the dirt. God continues to press His point: "Maybe he loves Me after all. Maybe he appreciates what My Son Jesus has already done. Maybe he's responding from love, rather
148

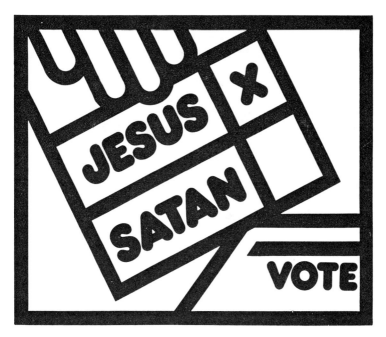

Is Satan correct in declaring that we seek God only to get things, or Jesus, when He says we seek Him out of love? Our devotional life—when things go bad—is our vote.

than trying to get more things from Me. Is this possible?"

By this time the devil has already begun to leave, because he has no answer. His only peace is in getting as far away as he can.

What has happened? I've cast my vote in favor of God. God is right and the devil flees from the scene as a defeated foe. This doesn't mean I'll never see him again. Anyone who has been fighting the good fight of faith knows that the devil refuses to give up. He'll return to try again. But as long as I continue to fellowship with God for His sake, then **He** is in control.

While this whole conflict would be somewhat vulgarized, I suppose, by a very human illustration, I'll try to use it, anyway. It's a scene between my teenage son and me.

One day he comes to me as I'm preparing to go on a journey. He says, "Looks like you're going on a trip today."

I answer, "Yes, Son, I am."

"Well, I'd like to go with you. May I?"

Inwardly I'm overjoyed. Deep down inside I've been worried about the communication gap that has been growing between my son and me. I say to myself, "Well, look at that! My teenage son wants to go with me on my journey. He must like me!"

I say to him, "Sure, come along. I'd like to have you with me."

We get in the car and start down the road. After a few pleasant miles, he says, "Dad?"

"Yes?"

"There's something I need."

"Really? What is it?"

"I need a new motorcycle."

Suddenly the entire picture jumps together in one dismal scene. I can't miss it—it's so clear. He wanted to go on a trip with me so he could ... yup ... I see. I reply, "I'm sorry, Son. We can't get you a new motorcycle right now. We can't afford it."

"Why not?"

"Because I said we don't have the money."

"But I need it!"

And we exchange words back and forth for a while, then the silence sets in. It grows heavy and stays all day. The trip is very long and tense. I don't look his way—I look out my side of the car while he looks out the other side. Finally, after long, excruciating hours, we are back home again. He goes to bed without even saying "Good night." I go to bed and lie awake, staring at the ceiling, wondering what's going to happen between my teenager and me.

Now, let's redo the scene to the ideal setting.

My son comes to me and says, "Dad, I understand you're going on a trip today. I'd like to come along, if you'll let me."

"Oh, wonderful!" (My boy likes me!)

We start down the highway. Everything is pleasant, and it remains that way. He doesn't ask me for special favors. He came along only because he likes his dad and the opportunity to fellowship with him. The communication is tremendous. We discuss everything—his joys, his sorrows, things that are happening to him. I share some of my problems with him, and we

When we spend time "beholding" Jesus, God unlocks our hearts, and we seek God for Himself, maturing beyond the self-centered reasons that motivated our early seeking.

communicate with each other all day long. The time goes by too quickly; it is soon over.

When we get home, he says, "Thanks, Dad, for letting me go with you. It's been wonderful. I had a great time."

Then he goes to bed, and I go into the family room where my wife is. I say to her, "Honey, I can't believe it. It was tremendous. We had a great time today—we just talked and fellowshiped. I wonder...do you think our son could use a new motorcycle?" And all of a sudden I have money that I didn't know I had.

Now, I don't want to force this illustration to "stand on all fours," because we'd run into the problem of anthropomorphism—dragging God down to our level and making Him into the type of God who gets His feelings hurt.

But if the God of love who created us can understand the thrill of being with someone who is communicating with Him simply for the joy of learning to know Him, rather than coming just to get things—even Heaven or solutions to problems—then, perhaps, we can understand why we'll continue to do worse when we pray, until we realize the right motive for seeking God. God can give us that motive only when we come to Him.

I need the right motive for seeking God, and I want to pray for the right motive, so that regardless of what happens in the future, I'll continue to seek Him because of His great manifestation of love at the Cross. Won't you join with me in seeking God because of gratitude for His gift of Jesus?

> Dear Father in Heaven, thank You for Your great heart of love, for sending Jesus to demonstrate it to us. We pray that You'll purify and transform our rotten motives. So often we've measured our salvation by looking at our own behavior and the circumstances around us. Deliver us from that trap, we pray. Please forgive us for this "on-again, off-again" communication with You, and teach us to know You as our personal Friend, so that we'll keep on coming every day, no matter what happens, in order to become acquainted with Jesus on a one-to-one basis, we pray, in Jesus' name, Amen.

10

How to Handle Temptation

I've frequently heard frustrated Christians admit, "I understand that if I'm focusing my time and effort in continuing my relationship with Christ, then He will take care of my sins. I realize that I'm not supposed to fight my own problems and **theoretically** if I'm surrendered to Christ, I will not sin. But it hasn't worked that way in experience; I find myself sinning even after I've spent time alone with Him in the morning. Do I have to wait until I'm 90 before I can have victory in my life? What am I supposed to do until then?"

Practical questions. And while some people might think this concern with sanctification is confined only to teenagers and boys and girls, I have met many kindly little white-haired grandmothers and other elderly people who have confessed this problem to be real in their lives, too.

If we could discover how to handle temptation according to God's way, and if we could learn to explain every facet of this topic so that it could be clearly understood, we would perhaps answer the most pressing questions that people have been asking. The little understanding that we have on the subject seems to have been discovered by accident, and, unfortunately, many cannot pass on to others the reasons for success in their own experiences.

What is our part in trying to handle sins, problems, and temptations that arise in the course of daily living? How much effort does God require of us before we can get victory over temptation?

I'd like to remind you, first of all, that if **we** try to handle our sins and temptations apart from God, we won't succeed. Anyone who tries to take care of these things through his own techniques, methods, and gimmicks is going to lose the battle. I'd also like to suggest that each person's method of handling temptations, prior to his understanding of our proper role in Christian living, has probably been influenced by the amount of will power that he happens to have (or by the amount he lacks). The question of how to handle temptation is a composite of all the facets of righteousness by faith in Christ alone. It is the personal application of the theory in the individual crisis.

As we begin to study this topic, I'd like to emphasize that sin is not confined to the area of behavior—doing wrong things. According to Romans 14:23, "whatsoever is not of **faith** is sin." Therefore the greatest single sin (which **causes** all other sins) and the primary issue in temptation is to do whatever we do, right or wrong, **outside of the faith relationship with Christ**. When we're living apart from Him, from dependence upon Him, then the **sins**—doing wrong things—automatically follow as a **result**. If my problem seems to be with committing sins, my real problem is back at the primary issue of dependence on God—whether I am living the life of faith or whether I am relying upon my own strength.

That's why the devil does everything he can to sever our connection with Christ. He knows that this relationship is the sum and total of the Christian life. He tempts us through our weaknesses, our problems, and our past failures, and once he gets our attention away from Christ, then he can finish us off with one of his big guns.

The Bible gives us some encouragement for genuine victory, for we are told that Jesus understands our problems and struggles.

> Seeing then that we have a great high priest, that is passed into the heavens, Jesus the Son of God, let us hold fast our profession. For we have not an high priest which cannot be touched with the feeling of our infirmities; but was in all points tempted like as we are, yet without sin. Let us therefore come boldly unto the throne of grace, that we may obtain mercy, and find grace to help in time of need—Hebrews 4:14-16.

This passage tells us that we have a great High Priest in

Jesus, our sympathetic High Priest in Heaven, was not tempted in every specific way we are (like watching murder mysteries on the "Late Late Show"), but to the extent that we are—and further.

Heaven—a real live person in human form in Heaven. What is He doing? He's remembering what it was like to live in our world of sin, and He knows what it means to be "touched with the feeling of our infirmities." When He was here on earth, He was tempted the same way we are today.

Now, He wasn't tempted to eat a triple-decker at Baskin-Robbins ice cream store five times a week. He wasn't tempted to watch murder mysteries on "The Late Late Show" on television. When the Bible says that He was tempted in "all points," it doesn't mean all the details of temptations that we have today. Hot rods would have been chariots in His day! Reading the comic strips in my day seems to be the equivalent of using marijuana today. Through the centuries, there seems to be an evolution in terms of sins and temptations and the things that

155

clamor for our attention, but the basic principle behind all sins and temptations remains the same. The person who tries to figure out how Jesus could possibly have been tempted in all the little things that we have to face today is going too far. I would like to add that "all points" does not appear in the original Greek text; it merely says that Jesus was tempted in "all." But He was tempted to every extent and was probably tempted even further than we ever will be, yet He did not sin.

Because Jesus is our great example of how to live, it would help to know how He overcame temptations. What did He have to say on the subject? He was in the garden of Gethsemane just before His arrest and trial. His disciples were supposed to keep Him company, but they were getting drowsy; they were having trouble staying awake. And Jesus said to them, "Pray that you won't enter into temptation .... Why are you sleeping? arise and pray, so you won't enter into temptation"—Luke 22:40, 46. Do you see the sequence at all? Pray **now**—**before** temptation comes.

The book of Matthew describes the same scene with slightly different wording: "Watch and pray, **that** you enter not into temptation: the spirit indeed is willing, but the flesh is weak"—Matthew 26:41. Now, some people will say, "That's the secret! I'm supposed to watch against temptation, and at the first sign of trouble, I'll pray and gain the victory."

No, I don't believe that's what Jesus taught. The sequence is to pray **before** temptation ever appears. Isn't that what Jesus was saying? "Watch and pray"—**now**, "that you won't enter into temptation"—**later**. "Let us come boldly before the throne of grace"—**now**, "that we might have help in time of need"—**then**. Does this make sense to you?

I believe that we have been defeated in our attempts to live the Christian life because in a crisis, we try to draw on reserve power that we don't have. We forget that we don't write a check unless we have money in the bank to cover the check. And when we do write a check without having reserve in the bank, it bounces. May I suggest to you that genuine victories over temptations are **always** won long before the temptations hit? If you rely for victory solely upon something that you do at the moment temptations come, you'll fail.

The apostle Paul emphasized the need to have power **before** temptation strikes when he said, "The Lord knows how

When we try to "handle" our sins and temptations ourselves—through whatever techniques, methods, or gimmicks—we have destined our efforts to failure.

to deliver the godly out of temptations"—II Peter 2:9. Notice that you have to be among the godly before you can be delivered, and remember that being godly is more than simply being a member of the church. We should know that much by now! Judas was a member of the church; he was even a church treasurer. Ananias and Sapphira were members of the church. Being godly includes something more than external morality when others are looking. It goes beyond merely paying tithe, being staunch health reformers, or giving your property to the church. Some of the best people in terms of moral behaviorists—church leaders, in fact—put Jesus on the cross. Being godly is impossible apart from knowing God and from being a partaker of His godliness.

Would it be safe to say that the Lord is not able to deliver the ungodly out of temptation? Why can't He? When people say that God can do **anything**, they forget that He has given us freedom of choice. God can't change my life for me unless I ask Him. Because of the great controversy between good and evil in the universe, He has voluntarily limited Himself when it comes to changing my life. The nature of His kingdom is not force; He never crowds us. We must **choose** to come under His control of love. And if we do not choose to rely on God, then He cannot help us handle temptations. Only when we have allowed Him to bring us into the experience of being spiritual (rather than just religious) can He deliver us out of temptations. In other words, the great God who created and now controls the sun, moon, stars, and all the planets and keeps them from crashing together, the God who sustains all life throughout the universe, the God who could hang a world of six sextillion tons on nothing—that same God can do nothing to change my life unless I allow Him to.

Often we have gone through the Bible, seeking promises that we can claim for help in time of trouble, ignoring the conditions listed right in those promises. One such text is found in I Corinthians 10:13:

> No temptation has taken you except that which is common to man: but God is faithful, who will not allow you to be tempted above that you are able; but will with the temptation also make a way of escape, that you may be able to bear it.

Is this text for just **anybody** who wants to claim it? Wasn't Paul talking only to godly people? Perhaps Paul was being a little too gracious toward the Christians at Corinth, but he was assuming that his readers knew what it meant to be spiritual, to be godly, and to have a faith relationship with God. And I do not believe that this promise can apply to a person who is living apart from this relationship.

Now, we've all heard of various remedies that are suggested to people for overcoming temptations. Have you ever tried any of these? I've tried all of them, but they haven't worked. I don't believe that praying when temptations come is going to give me victory. I've tried it, and it doesn't work. I don't believe that
158

**The example of Jesus in dealing with temptation
was always to "watch and pray" before the pressure
was on; every genuine victory over temptation is won
long before the moment of crisis comes.**

quoting verses of Scripture when temptations come is going to give me victory over temptation. I've tried that, too, and it doesn't work. I don't believe that singing hymns is effective, either, because I've tried all 16 stanzas! And usually when people try these methods, they become frustrated and discouraged, because failure and defeat still come. The problem is that they are fighting the battle where the battle isn't.

Because we have not realized that victory can come only through our relationship with Christ, we have devised all these man-made substitutes. I recall hearing someone discuss actual cases which "proved" that the solution was to pray **when** temptations strike. He told of a man who was angry with another man; he was ready to smash the other in the face. His eyes were bulging; his neck was red; his veins were standing out. But just before he pasted the other guy in the mouth, he came to the realization that he was being tempted. And the counsel was that when he came to that point of realization, he should pray. Really? He should have prayed a long time before he got to that point!

Suppose I'm standing in line at Baskin-Robbins for the fifth time this week, ready to order a triple-decker. (That's the vegetarian way of getting drunk, you know!) There I am. The attendant has already put the scoops on, I have the cone in my hand, and I'm all ready to take a bite. Suddenly I realize that I am struggling with temptation. Strange that I didn't recognize the temptation before I reached this stage of it! Haven't I already lost the battle over the primary issue? If so, an exercise of will power at that point might help me to stop from carrying out the deed, but it won't give me genuine victory because all **true** obedience comes from the heart.

You see, there are two points to remember—1) The real issue in sin and temptation is dependence upon myself, and 2) if I am depending on myself, then I'll usually resort to certain gimmicks and maneuvers to get myself out of the crisis I'm already in. Even if I do manage to stop from carrying out the actual temptation, the "victory" is only external. God's plan is for us to resist the primary issue in sin and temptation by fighting the fight of faith—knowing what it means to depend upon God. And in this relationship of faith, there is money in the bank. Then when the temptations come, **God** handles them for me.

The problem is, however, that the "stubborn Dutchman" type of person—the one who is able to handle the temptations outwardly apart from his relationship of dependence—fools himself into thinking that he is handling the temptations adequately. But remember, sin and temptation are stronger than any man's will power, and if I think I have enough backbone to overcome the real issue of temptation myself, then I'm being self-deceived. The only thing that I can do with my **backbone** in handling temptations is to **appear** victorious on the **outside**. But I've already lost the battle on the inside. True, ultimate victory is always from within **before** the crisis ever reaches me. The victory doesn't come at the time of the crisis.

"Well," says someone, "Jesus quoted Scripture when He was being tempted, and that's how he got victory over the devil." Jesus did quote Scripture, but that is **not** the way He got victory.

160

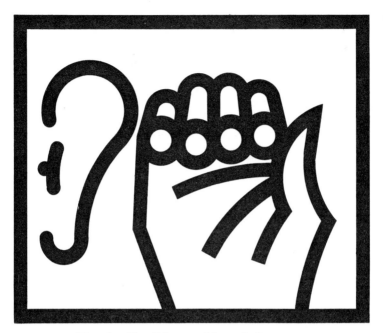

**The devil's whispered temptations are
ineffective on the "godly." They may react by praying,
reading Scripture, or singing hymns, but these actions
do not provide victory—they overcome
because they are "godly."**

It is very interesting to read the account of His temptation in the wilderness. "Then Jesus was led up **of the Spirit** into the wilderness to be tempted of the devil"—Matthew 4:1. Jesus was guided by the Spirit. He was willing to let God lead His life and actions.

Now, some have said that the real issue in the temptation was appetite, and that Jesus won over His appetite by quoting the Scriptures. But is it a sin to be hungry when you haven't eaten for six weeks? No. The devil's first front of temptation was **not** to get Jesus to eat. The issue was entirely different. It was to get Jesus to do something on His own, by Himself, using His inherent divinity, rather than to rely upon His Father's power. If He had yielded to the devil's taunts, He would have ruined the demonstration that He came to give as to how we should live, as to how we should handle temptations.

Jesus didn't fall into the devil's traps. His constant response was, "It is written..." but some have used this experience to support the idea that we must memorize Scripture to get us out of difficulty. Did Jesus **depend** upon the quoting of Scripture for victory? No! Let's explore this possibility a little more.

Have you ever been in a situation in which you were being tempted, and in which you felt that if you quoted Scripture, it might help—but you didn't quote Scripture, because you didn't want help at that point?

Let's suppose you were being tempted with getting a triple-decker at Baskin-Robbins. You're afraid that if you prayed, God might manage to stop you from carrying through with the temptation. So you save your prayer until later, when you ask for forgiveness. I'm speaking from personal experience.

Then there's the kind of temptation in which you don't have any time to pray or quote Scripture. Some temptations require careful planning, thought, and premeditation on your part—the long form. But the short form of temptation is quicker—you slap me, I slap you back. There's no time to quote Bible verses. No time to pray. No time to sing hymns. And if you're ever going to get any help over the short-form temptations, you'll have to have the reserve in the bank before the temptations ever hit you. Does that make any sense? And really, is there any difference **in principle** between the short-form and the long-form temptations? No difference. The long form occurs when someone suggests, "Let's go to Baskin-Robbins next week. I'll meet you there." The only difference is that you have all week to plan it. (And please don't stay away from Baskin-Robbins because of my illustration!)

Then why did Jesus quote Scripture if it wasn't to get victory? The quoting of Scripture was a spontaneous response to the crisis of the moment. He had already known the use of Scripture on His knees in secret prayer—long before the crisis with Satan in the wilderness, and He knew what it was like to have the exceeding riches of the grace and power of God in His life. He didn't depend upon victory from God's indwelling presence which resulted from His daily personal relationship with the Father. A person **may** pray when he is tempted, if he is in touch with the Father, he **may** quote Scripture, he **may** sing, but that's **not** what gives him victory over the temptation. Is that clear at

We can't write a check unless we have money in the bank; we can't call on God's power to resist temptation in the face of an "emergency" unless we've been in daily communion with Him.

all?

It is true that Jesus told us to watch and pray. But He wasn't talking primarily about watching for temptations on specific things. We need to watch that nothing will separate or keep us from God, from our personal dependence, from the daily relationship with Him. Only then can we have victory. **Steps to Christ** puts it this way:

Christ made a way of escape for us. He lived on earth amid trials and temptations such as we have to meet. He lived a sinless life. He died for us, and now He offers to take our sins and give us righteousness (p. 62).

How does our dependence upon Christ give us the victory

163

over sins? What does our relationship with God accomplish?

> Christ changes the heart. He abides in your heart by faith. You are to maintain this connection with Christ by faith and the continual surrender of your will to Him; and **so long as you do this**, He will work in you to will and to do according to His good pleasure .... Then **with Christ working in you**, you will manifest the same spirit and do the same good works—works of righteousness, obedience—**Ibid.**, pp. 62, 63 (emphasis supplied).

This same principle is taught in Hebrews 4:16, but many of us have misunderstood and misused the meaning of the text. If we were to read it the way we've often practiced in handling temptations of our own, we would read it as follows: "Let us come boldly to the throne of grace **in time of need** that we may obtain mercy." But it doesn't say that! It says, "Let us therefore come boldly unto the throne of grace, that we may obtain mercy, **and** find grace to help **in time of need**"—Hebrews 4:16. Do you see the difference between the two ways of reading this verse?

I have already mentioned a bank from which we can draw reserve power. The exceeding riches of the grace of God and our Lord Jesus Christ make any billionaire here on earth look like a pauper! Is there a mighty bank of Heaven from which we may draw? Yes! If we know what it means to keep in touch with the great Banker of Heaven, then when the crisis comes, the power will be there for us. Isn't that true? And I'd like to know more about keeping in constant touch with the **source** of that power.

"Well," says someone, "then you're really saying that God can only deliver the godly out of temptation, and so if I fall into temptation, then I'm not godly."

Is this correct? In a sense, yes! I wasn't relying on God at that time; so I fell. The Lord knows how to deliver me from temptation at the times when I'm depending on Him rather than myself, even while I'm trying to learn what it means to be "godly" or dependent on Him **all** of the time.

In other words, I can know ultimate victory whenever I am depending on Him. (There is no such thing as partial surrender, for at any moment, I am either totally depending upon God or totally upon myself.) Therefore I don't have to wait until I'm 90 before I can experience victory over sins. It can happen at any moment that I fully surrender to Him, even at the beginning of my Christian experience, for growth in the process of sanctification is in the **constancy** of my surrender to His control of love.

Then just because I fail in a given temptation doesn't mean that I don't still belong to God. It does indicate, however, that in some sense, because I'm an immature Christian, I am not depending upon Him at the time, but am depending, instead, upon myself and some fancy maneuvers to get me out of the crisis. When I realize that I have sinned, I don't waste any time in coming back to God immediately in repentance. And if I'll continue to seek Him regardless of my failures, He'll see me through to complete and ultimate, continuous victory.

That's the significance of the text that says, "Whosoever abides in him does not sin: whosoever sins has not seen him, neither known him"—I John 3:6. I've heard some say that this text means we won't sin **habitually**, but no one has yet told me when a sin becomes a **habit**. If I get an ice cream cone at Baskin-Robbins once a year, is that a habit? Do I have to get ice cream at Baskin-Robbins every December 31? If I eat a triple-decker once a month? Or is it a habit only if I do it five times a week? I defy you to tell me what habitual sinning would be, if sin is defined in terms of behavior alone.

What does the text really mean? It is telling us that the primary issue in sin is **not abiding in Him**. Then if I **am** abiding in Him, I'm not sinning. When I'm not abiding in Him, I'm sinning. Verse 9 of John 3 tells us that "anyone who has been born of God does not commit sin, for Jesus, the Word of God, abides in him: and he cannot sin, because he is born of God." When I have been born again, when I've been converted, I don't want to live on my own independence. I will want to qualify for what it means to abide in Christ, to come under His control of love. That's the basic issue in sin, the primary issue in **any** temptation—to do whatever I do apart from dependence on Him.

Remember that God never intended that we should be obsessed with our sins, our mistakes, or our problems. If we focus on them, the devil is assured of victory. God's plan is better. It is to look to Him, to consider Him, and to know Him in a personal, daily relationship of love and dependence. This direction of the will is the proper way to handle temptation.

I'm thankful for the example Jesus gave and for the experiences of people who have learned and who are still learning the truth of how to handle temptation. I've been encouraged by one writer who shares his experience with us in these words:

> For a long time I tried to gain victory over sin, but I failed. I have since learned the reason. Instead of doing the part which God expects me to do, and which I can do, I was trying to do God's part, which He does not expect me to do, and which I cannot do. Primarily, my part is **not to win the victory**, but to **receive** the victory which has already been won for me by Jesus Christ.

Can you identify with him? He continues:

> This victory is inseparable from Christ Himself, and when I learned how to receive Christ as my victory through **union** with Him, I entered upon a new experience. I do not mean to say that I have not had any conflicts, and that I have not made any mistakes. Far from it. But my conflicts have been when influences were brought to bear upon me to induce me to lose my confidence in Christ as my personal Saviour, and to **separate** from Him ....
>
> The fight which I am to fight is 'the good fight of faith. I do not believe in myself, and therefore I have no confidence in my own power to overcome evil. I hear Him saying to me, 'My power is made perfect in weakness,' and so I surrender my whole being to be under His control, allowing Him to work in me 'both to will and to work' .... He does not disappoint me. **By living His life of victory in me, He gives me the victory.**—W. W. Prescott, **Victory in Christ**, Review and Herald Publishing Association, pp. 25-27.

I would like to appeal to you, my friend, to learn what it means to come before the throne of grace when the pressure isn't on, **before** the crisis arises, when the devil isn't facing you with temptations. That's what Jesus did—He spent those quiet, early hours of each morning with God, seeking strength for the day. That's the only way we can have victory!

I'll never forget the day this truth dawned on me. I had been studying this subject of victorious living, and I was beginning to conclude that the entire process of sanctification was based on the ongoing fellowship and relationship with Jesus. It looked too good to be true. I could hardly believe it could be that simple. And I remember asking God for a sample that morning: "Please, Lord, this sounds like the answer. I think I understand the theory, but I need to experience it as well. Please give me an example of it today."

I went about my work and forgot all about that prayer until noon, when I was driving down a busy street in Sacramento. Suddenly a temptation of the flesh hit me, and at the moment it did, there was a cold shiver like an electric shock that ran over me, and that didn't make sense, because it was a hot summer day. Evidently my revulsion at the temptation caused the cold shiver. At the same moment, the temptation was gone, and even though I momentarily tried, I couldn't remember what it was. It was like some kind of amnesia.

Maybe this experience sounds weird to you, but I don't think it was. You might explain it as some sort of psychological preconditioning, but I cannot. I knew that my contact with God that morning had been valid, and I knew God was with me at the time of the temptation. I remember pulling over to the curb. I couldn't keep the tears back as I bowed my head and asked God to help me never forget that moment, and to help me share the basis of that experience with others. I believe that God in His great love gave me, right then, a sample of what ultimate victory can be, to encourage me in answer to my prayer. I wish I could say that every moment of every day since that time has been like that, but like everyone else, I've had to go through the painful struggle of growth and learning to depend more and more constantly upon God and less and less on my own gimmicks.

I'm thankful for the great God of Heaven who has promised to handle our temptations for us, who has promised to supply the power we don't have. I'm thankful for Jesus who made victory possible by His life of victory and by His death on the cross. I want to know more of depending on Him, of abiding in Him every moment of every day. Don't you?